Mentoring
for Talent

Mentoring for Talent

A Practical Guide for Schools

Mark A. Smith

Published in 2024 by Amba Press, Melbourne, Australia
www.ambapress.com.au

Cover design: Tess McCabe
Internal design: Amba Press
Editor: Andrew Campbell

ISBN: 9781923116764 (pbk)
ISBN: 9781923116771 (ebk)

A catalogue record for this book is available from the National Library of Australia.

Contents

About the author

Mark Smith is an innovative educator with over 30 years' experience in the Victorian independent school system. He holds a Master of Education in gifted and talented education from Monash University, Melbourne, and has long been associated with the Victorian Association for Gifted and Talented Children (VAGTC), where he also served as president between 2018 and 2021.

His work in gifted and talented education has seen Mark create and implement multifaceted school-wide programs at some of Melbourne's largest independent schools. An advocate for guided inquiry-based learning approaches, Mark has facilitated outstanding academic results for students of all ages, using mentoring to cultivate questioning skills and deep, engaging personal research processes, often leading to student agency and transformational learning.

The personalised nature of mentoring combines many of Mark's passions in education, including relationship-building, fostering a sense of belonging, goal-setting, formative feedback, progress-checking, questioning, trouble-shooting and high-interest action research – all techniques that support the whole person in their development.

Mark is adamant about building the learning scaffold for all students and he uses mentoring as one means of achieving this. In his broader work, he has advocated for every student being presented with the opportunity to embrace their best learning at their developmental stage so that they can perform in all areas – academic, social/emotional and personal – in line with their abilities.

In addition to mentoring, Mark uses a range of real-life enrichment techniques in his teaching, including research and problem-solving. Depending on the learning context, he encourages his students to work individually, in small groups, and using collaborative approaches to engage, motivate and enable best outcomes. This creative, relevant and high-interest approach to teaching and learning incorporates significant differentiation at the highest level of student ability, promoting learning for life and inspiring students to perform at the peak of their achievement capabilities.

Ultimately Mark hopes that his students will be transformational in their learning, using their skills and abilities for the good of others and to make a positive difference in society. Again, mentoring provides a role-modelled process for this development and transformation.

Mark is married to Kristen, another passionate educator. He has two adult children, Jordan and Charlotte. He lives on a small acreage at Warrandyte in Melbourne. Mark has an appreciation of nature and the environment, and in his spare time enjoys coastal fishing and exploration, something he makes time for regularly along the vast Gippsland coast of Victoria.

Introduction

Growing up in a small country town in Gippsland in the late seventies, I attended a tiny country school with about 75 primary students. It is fair to say that my educational experience started very small. Differentiation was not a term I had ever heard of, and the only ability grouping I could ever remember was in spelling, where we had mauve-coloured books with levels from 1 to 30. Students started at Level 1 with the most basic of words, and in time, through a practice and testing process, they hoped that they might get to Level 30, where the words were much harder to spell.

I guess to some extent reading was also set by ability, starting with Dick and Dora, and Fluff and Nip, then moving to the Victorian Readers First Book to Sixth Book, then branching boldly into the Enid Blyton or Dr Seuss series. I was never much of a reader, so I did not care much for the books or the progression in which they were read. I recall taking a long time to even get through my very first reader, so my reading must have taken a long time to develop.

However, I do remember sport at school, and the relationships I had with my teachers. In fact, it was my relationships with my teachers and peers that enabled me to enjoy primary school so much. I lived for sport, and even in our tiny country school we still had inter-school sport. The boys played football (VFL) back then, and the girls played netball, and students worked hard from Year 3 to gain a place in the teams that competed against other schools each Friday afternoon. Our teachers were the coaches and umpires, and we had the best time playing and competing. We also participated in swimming and athletics, where we competed against six to eight other schools of similar size on big carnival days. Even back then, if we performed well, we could qualify for District, then Regionals, then State competition, if we continued to progress.

In the small town we would often see our teachers on the weekend playing footy or netball, at the local dance, or just passing by in the street. The teachers were part of our community and we adored them. I was not a quick learner at that time, but I did integrate well into school, and I was swept up in the very basic educational culture of my tiny school. I learned almost by osmosis rather than anything very strategic or specific. For me, it was the very act of joining in and having a go that enabled me to develop new skills. I was struck by the humour of the teachers and my peers and the bonds we formed. We kind of just learned together with very little stress or pressure. As I look back, it was actually very special.

It is interesting that I remembered these student/teacher relationships and this positive school culture from my primary experience when it came to my own teaching. When I was trying to solve a learning problem with my gifted and high-ability primary students at a large independent school in Melbourne 15 years later, I was drawn back to what had enabled me as a student to learn best during my primary years. First and foremost, I knew that it was connection and relationship.

Much had changed: not only was I a qualified teacher, but I was now a specialist educator with post-graduate qualifications in gifted education working in a large school of 2000 students. In this state-of-the-art educational setting, it is hard to believe that much could have been learned from the educational experience I had enjoyed in my tiny rural primary school, yet that could not be further from the truth. It was those memories of my primary experience that enabled me to look creatively at how I might be able to solve the problem before me.

The problem was: how to engage my gifted and highly able primary students in inquiry learning tasks enabling them to:

• Devise an open research question

- Engage in research to address that question
- Work through a meaningful process of setting goals and checking progress
- Create a sequence of tasks that enabled measurement of those question-based goals
- Include some analysis of those measurements, and
- Reach some well-researched conclusions.

It was a complex challenge, yet I firmly believed that teacher intervention and support, and a shared connection between student and teacher, could achieve such learning targets.

There started my research of mentoring processes, and my discovery of a whole new world of highly effective teaching and differentiated action, which transformed me as a teacher and a learner.

This book explores that research, and all that has unfolded as a result, including my master's research, which concluded in 2009, and my new understanding of school culture and how this can be enhanced through mentor/mentee engagements. It also provides an alternative avenue for student engagement and student/teacher connection – an alternative that can be practical and effective, particularly following the recent Covid-19 pandemic when this engagement and connection was so sorely impacted.

My story of practical mentoring spans two decades of tried practice, and much of it is shared in this book. I am still amazed by what I have learned and what has taken place, but no one could question the extraordinary successes of the mentees in the many facets of mentorship and afterwards. From winning national academic competitions, both individually and collaboratively, sharing their stories at world conferences, reaching the highest levels of achievement in a range of academic and sporting domains, to perfect scores in the Victorian Certificate of Education (VCE).

I am extremely grateful for the opportunities I have had in education, and the freedom that my schools have afforded me in my teacher practice. Much can be said for a school that provides its teachers with a position description, then largely empowers its staff to enhance it. In fields such as gifted education where the skills and knowledge required are so specialised, much trust is required on the part of senior management, who need to rely on the integrity of their experts. This trust has enabled me to provide amazing opportunities for my student mentees, and these opportunities have led to their extraordinary achievements.

This is a story of mentorship that I felt needed to be told. It has been written to:

1. Support teacher mentors as they embark on different ways of creating positive connection with their students, supporting them socially, emotionally, and academically
2. Assist school leaders with strategies for student improvement – personally, within the well-being space, and academically
3. Provide school leaders with an avenue for promoting positive school culture and dramatically improving student academic outcomes.

I am confident that reading this book will open your eyes to what can be achieved in this educational space, and the vast possibilities of creative strategy in future teacher practice.

Chapter 1

Why mentoring?

"A great mentor helps one to achieve what seems impossible."
– Mariela Dabbah

Having worked in education for 32 years and having witnessed the abilities of many teachers in a variety of contexts, I have found that the best teachers demonstrate active, engaged and relational mindsets. The best teachers proactively seek to advance the abilities of their students, enabling them to take guided steps towards being their best selves. These teachers are naturally curious themselves and on behalf of their students, they use time well, have learned from their own experience, have a degree of wisdom, and are highly strategic. In their daily teaching they are active observers scanning for gaps or areas of deficit to address within their classrooms. When a problem presents itself, they are ready to act. This action initially might be further observation, as students can solve many of their own problems. Alternatively, it might be an active intervention. A good teacher will know the best course of action and be timely in their response.

A good teacher impacts every student

The teacher will impact every student in their class during every lesson of the day. It is important for the teacher to realise that this impact can be positive or negative. It is critical that the teacher quickly ascertains the needs of each student in their care for the students to engage with the lesson. Some students need to feel a sense of belonging before they are comfortable enough to engage, some may have a learning gap or deficit, or a processing issue leading to varying rates of retention, and others will pick up new concepts quickly, requiring extension and greater levels of challenge and complexity. The role of the teacher is a challenging one, as teachers need to be highly responsive and proactive to the needs of all students and to determine receptively and intuitively what is the best approach for the students before them.

Gone are the days when a teacher walks into the classroom, sits in the corner, and barks instructions at the class. Gone are the days of the "sage on the stage", as described by McWilliam (2009), where the teacher fills students like vessels with knowledge and information that they will retain for future reference. A minority of students might learn this way, but the vast majority will not. These are antiquated methods. Not only does the teacher need to determine the social and emotional position of each student, but they also need to ascertain preferred ways of learning and respond accordingly.

A good approach is to start with an enthusiastic teacher welcome, to determine some learning intentions, and to commence with perhaps 10 minutes or so of well-thought-out and creatively presented direct teaching, to set a context for the lesson. What comes next will be an action response to this direct teaching on the part of the student, be it individually, in pairs, or in a small group. The action response might involve reading, writing, listening or speaking. It might involve technology; it might involve collaboration and research. These are just some of the varying ways of learning that the students might engage with.

The response needs to address success criteria, or a learning target set by the teacher, and each individual student needs to know the part they are playing. The response will be short-term, but it might also contribute to a longer-term response. The teacher might act as McWilliam (2009) describes as a "guide on the side", stopping at frequent intervals to add some pearls of wisdom or guide the misguided or confused. This guidance can provide value as a class is finding its way, and it may assist with keeping all students on track. Better still, as McWilliam (2009) highlights, is the teacher serving as the "meddler in the middle", who "meddles" rather than guides. The meddler provides thoughts and provocations, an idea, or a perspective at critical times in the learning engagement. Students may or may not take up the meddle, but it will have been offered. The meddler in the middle promotes individual and group thinking and direction on the part of the students but still enables them to direct their own path and response. This action response is the application in practical terms of students to the direct teaching that came in the beginning.

For the last 10 minutes of the lesson there should be a student response through some oral sharing, written responses provided possibly via technology, or some discussion around questions that further enhance the lesson. All students should have played a role, and each should have a takeaway from the lesson. Each student will have engaged in the lesson using a combination of their own preferred ways of learning while also dabbling in a less preferred way. Some personal growth should have occurred and some progress on the lesson focus. Students should leave the class feeling they have had a degree of ownership and choice, and a level of meaningful engagement.

This is learning in action, students on task, and what we know as building the knowledge or skill scaffold for students. It is a constructivist approach where students build on prior knowledge, but some students will still underachieve or slip through the net, so other methods of support need to be considered and used.

Addressing underperformance creatively

When the school I was working in was presented with an issue related to student underperformance, my attention was raised. I immediately went into creative mode and started to consider ways of solving the problem for our students and the school.

The context was a large inquiry-based competition run by a Maths Association. Students were invited to submit individual or group entries for this competition. They were encouraged to enter a research project on a topic of their choice involving maths. The school had been entering this competition for a few years. While students had enthusiastically started their maths research by coming up with a topic and researching their chosen focus using the parameters provided by the association, no students had won any awards or achieved notable success as measured by the school. To make matters worse, many of the competitor schools were issuing press releases or earning accolades for their high-quality entries from the Maths Association through public announcements about specific school awards.

As the person leading gifted and talented programs in the school where I was employed and having a post-graduate qualification in the gifted and talented field, I was considered a person who might be able to help. I was still relatively new to the gifted and talented field, but I was young and enthusiastic, and I had some good ideas. Hence, I was approached by management to brainstorm some possible solutions.

I was a good teacher and I had confidence in my abilities with students, but most of my experience had been as a classroom teacher of upper primary students. My success as a teacher had stemmed from my ability to relate to students and to get them to successfully relate well to one another. I had the ability to make most students feel relaxed in my classroom, to feel part of the team that they formed as a class. I knew how to set up a positive culture where class members would look out for each other, learn together, and understand and appreciate the different skills and abilities that each class member had. I was highly organised, and I had good processes in place. I provided constructive feedback to students on their learning, and most students worked to respond to that feedback, growing as learners and personally as individuals.

I worked with a skilful team of educators who promoted similar cultures in their classrooms, and the school that I was working in had a positive and harmonious vibe. Students were generally happy and healthy. Why then were they not high-achieving in the Maths Association context? Was it a time issue or a focus issue? Did students not fully understand the gravity of the inquiry tasks and the rigour needed to address them well? These were some of my questions.

The students had some great project ideas, and the Maths Association had provided a good set of guidelines. Great starts were made, but the students' progress would inevitably fizzle. To me there was a breakdown in process, a lack of long-term task commitment, a struggle to maintain rigorous engagement. Deep down I believed that some one-to-one support was required to enable the process to maintain its momentum, support that would sustain what I knew our students were capable of. However, at that stage I wasn't sure how this might work or how it could be timetabled.

How might a good teacher solve a performance problem for students and the school?

In 2005 I was fortunate to win a professional development scholarship at my school. This scholarship enabled me to travel to the US and, among other things, attend a world gifted conference in New Orleans. At a pre-conference workshop I was able to attend a session run by Joyce VanTassel-Baska, a world leader in gifted education. As part of this workshop, mentoring was discussed, and VanTassel-Baska (2005a) highlighted how mentoring really is a non-negotiable need for gifted and talented students in a range of contexts. She shared that a strong misconception in the field of gifted and talented education is that gifted and talented children will always manage on their own because they are gifted or talented. This is not the case. In fact, due to their giftedness or talent, these students often have challenges in other areas, including organisational or executive functioning skills and social skills. These challenges often mask their abilities, leading to an inability to plan and an inability to discuss their ideas or collaborate at a high level.

Having worked in the learning skills unit at my school, I had seen first-hand the benefits that a specific and targeted learning support program could have for students with learning difficulties. I had seen how students with auditory processing deficits, short-term memory challenges, executive functioning issues, and other literacy difficulties could be helped with specific support programs. I had also led the charge on helping students with fine motor difficulties through administering a Beery Assessment (Beery et al., 2005), then addressing the recommendations provided in the individualised reports through targeted activities, practice, and repetition of key skills.

VanTassel-Baska, in the pre-conference workshop, was suggesting a similar type of intervention specific to gifted and highly able students to enable them to grow and thrive according to their skills and abilities. This was not something I had heard of before, and it went against the grain in terms of general funding support needs in schools, yet to me it made a lot of sense. Just because a student is gifted or has high ability should not disqualify them from support programs. Everyone deserves the chance to be their best selves, regardless of where they may start intellectually on the spectrum. This was a refreshing insight as far as I was concerned, and perhaps one that warranted further investigation. However, in terms of school priorities and the direction of resources, I was not sure that an intervention program for gifted and high-ability students could be justified in the eyes of management. Would they consider it fair and equitable?

In considering all of this, my judgement was that I had been afforded the invitation to weigh into the Maths Association underperformance issue, so here was an opportunity to determine and try a possible solution using a mentoring program. Surely a trial in the first instance would be supported, given the insights of a world leader in the field of gifted and talented education?

Gifted and high-ability learners will achieve much more with suitable support

Considering these insights on gifted and high-ability learners and VanTassel-Baska's thoughts in New Orleans, I felt a mentor could assist these gifted and talented students, so I set up a trial with 10 students for the maths competition the following year. The selected students covered a range of year levels from Year 2 to Year 6, and both boys and girls took part. Taking a lead from the learning skills unit team, I set up a well-planned approach to the mentoring and I used duplicate books to record all sessions so that the original copy of the session could be passed on to the student mentee, and so that the mentor could retain a carbon copy of each session for themselves. Mentoring sessions were set up weekly. Once the student's investigative idea had been determined and a plan had been created, an overarching question was developed. This overarching question was supported by a sequence of questions or tasks enabling full research. Weekly goals were then set for the student mentee, and progress checks were built in as part of each session.

Students who were thriving with their investigations were sometimes encouraged to increase the complexity of the task by modifying a question or adding a new element. Sometimes a new question was added. Similarly, students who were behind, or were struggling to grapple with the weekly tasks, were assisted in simplifying the research to make it more achievable. The flexibility to differentiate within the mentoring session was a definite highlight of the one-to-one sessions, and the student mentees maintained a high level of motivation and engagement in the process. All students were investigating an overarching question that they didn't know the answer to, and each was enthusiastic to collect data, measure and analyse data findings, and ultimately find answers to reach satisfying conclusions.

The relevance of Gagné's differentiated model of giftedness and talent

As I reflected on these newly formed mentorships and student investigations, I began to consider the latest model in gifted education, that of Françoys Gagné (2010), originally developed in 2003. I wanted to consider how Gagné's model might align with what I was setting out to do with my students.

This model not only helped make sense of giftedness and talent and how the talent development process works, it also enabled me to see how a mentoring program for gifted learners added significant learning value in a gifted student's developmental experience. The differentiated model of giftedness and talent in its latest version, as displayed in Figure 1, sets out this support process very logically in visual terms.

Figure 1: Gagné's differentiated model of giftedness and talent

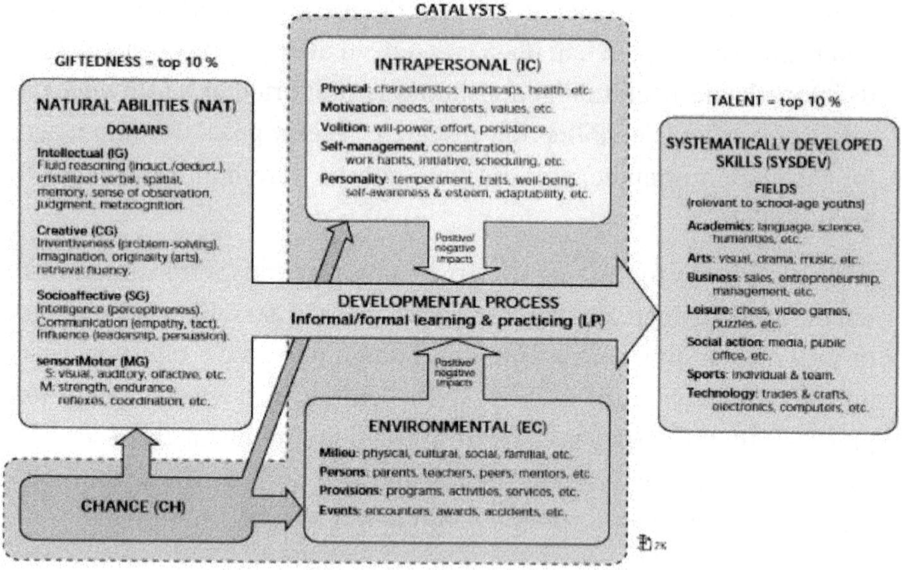

In understanding Gagné's talent development model, it is helpful to work through it from left to right. The model, starting at the top left, identifies the top 10% of individuals in a population as having gifted potential. This aptitude or potential expressed through natural abilities is what an individual is born with. It considers general intelligence, levels of creativity, social and emotional intelligence, and physical abilities. How this potential is nurtured is part of a broader developmental process that moves through the middle of the model. This development is influenced by Gagné's catalysts as outlined in the middle column and surrounded by a broken line. The catalysts impacting the developmental process are covered broadly by intrapersonal and environmental factors. Chance, which is often largely outside one's control, is also a catalyst.

Intrapersonal factors, which are driven and supported largely by the gifted individual, include:

- **Physical impacts** such as one's physical prowess and health
- **Motivation**, which is influenced by a person's values, as well as their needs and interests
- **Volition**, which relates to the drive, effort and persistence of the individual
- **Self-management**, which considers personal initiative, organisation and concentration
- **Personality**, which is driven by an individual's temperament, levels of well-being, self-esteem, and self-awareness.

These intrapersonal factors can be impacted in part by Gagné's environmental catalysts. **Environmental factors** in the model are broken down into four main categories, which are often initially outside the gifted individual's control. They include:

- **Milieu**, which considers a person's physical environment, their cultural influences, family arrangements and support, and social factors
- **Persons of influence**, including parents, teachers, mentors, and others within one's inner circle
- **Provisions**, which include an individual's access to programs, activities and services that might enrich a person and help them advance
- **Events**, which include life-changing encounters, awards or accolades which might lead to a life shift, good or bad.

The catalyst **chance** refers to those sliding door moments which could influence the direction of an individual either positively or negatively. Chance could include circumstances such as accidents, illnesses or injuries, an unexpected windfall, or an opportunity that is presented unexpectedly and not earned or influenced in any way. I often think that the words of the chorus of an Alanis Morissette (2015) song, "Ironic", capture chance quite well:

> *An old man turned ninety-eight*
> *He won the lottery and died the next day*
> *It's a black fly in your Chardonnay*
> *It's a death row pardon two minutes too late*
> *And isn't it ironic? Don't you think?*
> *It's like rain on your wedding day*
> *It's a free ride when you've already paid*
> *It's the good advice that you just didn't take*
> *And who would have thought? It figures.*

These lyrics express the challenges of life, the good or bad luck that can come one's way. Of course, how an individual responds to chance might also determine what comes next.

In considering Gagné's catalysts and their possible benefits to the developmental process, mentoring is included as an influence within the environmental catalysts. Therefore, it is supported by Gagné as being an experience of high benefit in enabling a gifted individual, as part of the developmental process, to move towards talent development as expressed through the systematically developed skills displayed in the right-hand column of Gagné's model.

For mentoring to demonstrate its potential benefit to an individual, it must be of high quality, sustained and purposeful to the recipient mentee. When a gifted person engages with high-quality mentoring in a purposeful activity, the environment catalyst is immediately enhanced, and opportunities for academic and personal growth are likely to be at the highest level. In fact, mentees should be able to work within their proximal zone of development (PZD), as described by Eun (2019), where an individual operates within the threshold of maximum challenge for their personal skill and knowledge capacity. The PZD was devised by Belarusian psychologist Lev Vygotsky during the late 1920s. It is a level of mentee challenge that mentors should strive for within the investigations and learnings of every mentorship.

Early signs of mentoring benefits and success

With my targeted intentions and the subsequent theoretical alignment, it should not come as any surprise that a well-planned mentoring trial with 10 students focusing on a maths investigation of choice, but also with significant challenge and interest, would see significant gains for the participants.

After eight weeks of well-planned differentiated mentoring was complete, and the student projects were assessed and put on display, the results were remarkable in terms of project depth, complexity and performance. Additionally, this new learning dimension paved the way for transformation of my teaching and learning approach and how teacher mentors can reach students in extraordinary ways.

This new learning dimension

Before commencing this new journey of student support, I had considered myself a good teacher. I had always been relational, well planned, and someone who considered the needs of everyone in my class. However, mentoring allowed me to drill down on each individual and to consider their personal academic needs according to their capability and readiness. All of the 10 mentored students achieved success in the Maths Association competition. All were selected to represent the school in the competition, and all won awards. Additionally, the school won an outstanding school award, an accolade reserved at that time for the top five schools in the competition. This was extraordinary considering that in previous years the school had not achieved a single award for any individual student or project. The mentoring had made a significant difference.

The following year, several mentored students in the school entered the Maths Association competition again, with 27 students winning awards, and an outstanding school award was again achieved. To demonstrate the transferrable nature of the mentoring process, that same year several mentored students were also entered in the Science Association competition, a competition that was very similar to the maths one, but a competition that the students in the school had never entered before. Thirty students entered the science competition, completing an investigative science project. Each was mentored using the same process as with the maths, and high-quality projects were completed. Twenty-seven projects were entered in the Science Association competition, and 18 high-level awards were won, including a prestigious Hugh McKnight school award acknowledging outstanding-quality entries schoolwide. Again, the mentoring had demonstrated its impact, albeit in a different context, that of science.

In years following, mentor support for gifted and high-ability students was set up for animation and movie-making competitions, and writing competitions, and similar results were attained. Not only did the students achieve far richer and satisfying investigations, but I too had become a highly effective mentor, and with it an even better teacher. Through the mentoring, I had been able to provide an outstanding environment for maximum learning and knowledge development, which had improved the academic achievements of each student, their confidence, and their belief in their ability to achieve. As a mentor, I was "systematically developing the skills" of my mentees, as seen in the right-hand column of Gagné's model (Figure 1), through multifaceted skill development on the part of the mentees. These systematically developed skills were transferable from one subject to another, or one discipline to another, and were enabling life-changing confidence, satisfaction and self-belief to be embedded in the mentees. Best of all, the mentees were achieving at a high level and were realising their potential through the authentic development of their talent.

In summary, the "Why mentoring?" question should now in part have been answered. In addition to the success of the initial mentoring trial, we also discovered that mentoring is supported and endorsed by key experts in the gifted field, including Joyce VanTassel-Baska (2005a, 2005b, 2007), who considers mentoring best practice for best outcomes. VanTassel-Baska also sees mentoring as a non-negotiable if gifted students are to achieve according to their potential. Further-more, mentoring is highlighted in Gagné's (2004) differentiated model of giftedness and talent as an important environmental factor in the talent development process. Gagné deemed it important enough to list mentoring by name within his model. With the support of such eminent theorists in the gifted field, it is exciting to then see how a well-planned mentoring process played out in one school to support gifted students addressing an underachievement issue. Exciting though it was, this was just the start. There is so much more still to uncover as we continue the journey through this transformative learning process that is mentoring.

So where to next?

In continuing this beneficial exploration, Chapter 2 will examine the differences between mentoring and coaching by way of definition and then in practical terms. As part of this, we will explore a case study where mentoring turned to coaching, and in doing so investigate why this was necessary and the subsequent outcomes of this adjustment.

Chapter 3 will delve into how mentoring can support student autonomy and agency, even with young primary students. Through this focus, we will uncover how this agency develops for student mentees, quite subconsciously at first in a primary setting.

In Chapter 4 we will look at the transferable nature of mentoring from mentor to mentee and from one subject or learning context to another. We will investigate how a similar mentoring structure can achieve a variety of productive learning applications for willing mentee participants.

The other mentoring applications that will be explored in detail in this book include, in Chapter 5, competition mentoring for inquiry projects. In this chapter we will examine how competition mentoring supports creative expression, task commitment, formative discussions around the progress of the goals, goal-setting and progress-checking within the inquiry project context. We will also learn about the benefits of this mentoring, which include research complexity, processes for learning, and outstanding student outcomes.

The other key mentoring focus will be in Chapter 6, where we will investigate in-depth academic mentoring with senior students in their last year of school. Benefits shared include improved work-life balance, organisation, goal-setting and progress-checking. Additionally, the benefits of social and emotional support, effective modes of communication, awareness and reflection, and outstanding academic outcomes will be explored.

In Chapter 7 the focus will be on authentic intentions and personal growth as we consider the mentoring participation of many gifted and high-ability learners over many years. We will investigate how the support of such programs has naturally enabled the developmental progression of some very wise, kind and transformational mindsets in students. Many of these student mindsets have the greater good in mind. How these mindsets have evolved or are evolving through these mentor programs will be analysed.

Chapter 8 will see us examining the benefits of caring mentor support, including how this has led to an open analysis of enrichment options enabling students to explicitly share their remarkable educational stories while developing a range of skills and leadership abilities.

Finally, in Chapter 9, we will examine the practical applications of facilitating mentor programs in schools. We will look at staff resourcing and timetabling and consider in detail how mentor programs can integrate effectively with broader school programs and build an academic culture of confidence and expectation that benefits all students above and beyond the gifted and highly able.

Discussion questions

1. What did you learn about mentoring by reading this chapter?
2. What did you learn about the development of gifted and talented students?
3. How might mentoring be of benefit to gifted and talented students?
4. How might mentoring be used to support all students in our context?

Where relevant, come up with two or three answers for each question.

Chapter 2

Mentoring or coaching?

"The greatest good you can do for another is not just to share your riches, but to reveal to them their own."

– Benjamin Disraeli

While mentoring and coaching share some common approaches, they are largely different disciplines.

Executive Coach International (n.d.) says that mentoring is predominantly directive and relies on the vast experience and expertise of someone usually much older to share by example the possibilities for future mentee achievement. Clasen and Clasen (2003) define mentoring as a situation where an older, more experienced person works with a younger person or protégé on teaching and training in a specific learning domain.

Coaching, on the other hand, is participatory. The coach could be less experienced and of a similar age to the coachee. The coach asks questions and prompts thinking and action on the part of the coachee.

Through coaching sessions, the onus is on the coachee being primed and conditioned to solve their own problems and self-monitor their progress and future actions.

The overlap lies in both practices involving intense listening, encouraging self-improvement, and providing a safe setting for honest sharing.

In this book, mentoring is the main focus, largely because in schools teacher mentors are more readily available. Teachers usually have relevant experience and expertise through the very act of completing their teacher training and teacher practice, and teachers are naturally directive in their approach. However, I am also a trained coach, having completed the senior growth coaching course with Growth Coaching International. This enables me to have a very open mind regarding my interactions with students. Hence, at times, particularly with older secondary students, the mentoring I conduct does include elements of coaching or will revert to coaching if that is deemed more suitable in the situation.

As part of this chapter, I will share a case study that provides a good example of where mentoring turned into coaching. This case study involves an older student who already had some established skills enabling them to fully utilise the coaching.

Key goals of mentoring

When I mentor a student, I have a few key goals in mind. Firstly, I want to get to know them as a person and develop a partnership of trust, as a positive relationship between mentor and mentee will likely enable more meaningful learning and a greater experience (Manning, 2006). I want to understand their background in education but also to some extent in life, as this will provide some context for their specific situation and needs. This includes establishing a picture of their interests and passions and gaining a clear view of their goals and what they wish to achieve at school and in life.

Secondly, influenced by Siegle and McCoach (2005), and their research on twice-exceptional gifted students, I work hard to gain an understanding of a student's ways of learning and any potential deficits or learning supports that they may require. For gifted and high-ability learners, these deficits are most likely to be social or organisational, but the mentee could also have learning challenges. Exploring deficits and working around these will be explored further in Chapter 3.

Once I have a clear view of the background and context of the mentee, and I have established an understanding of their learning style, together we consider the mentoring intentions of the partnership. Some examples of the mentoring intentions might include:

- To enable full mentee awareness of all pending tasks that need to be completed by the student with the dates for completion.
- To ensure the student reflects on their progress through progress-checking as discussed formatively with their mentor.
- To ensure mentees keep mentors informed of any challenges or concerns that they may have so that appropriate support can be provided.
- To ensure that mentees set considered, purposeful goals for the next stage of their work.

The mentoring intentions will be discussed at the beginning of the mentorship, and we will establish a mutual understanding regarding them. Following this discussion, the mentor and mentee will together look at the success criteria for the mentoring sessions. These will determine what we need to do together and as individuals in the partnership to ensure that success can most likely be achieved. An example of some success criteria might be:

- The mentee meets with their mentor regularly, preferably weekly.
- The mentee, with the support of their mentor as required, irons out any concerns or challenges they might have.
- The mentee shows their mentor in concrete terms that all goals (or at least most goals) have been achieved.
- The mentee reflects on their progress and considers this reflection formatively in setting their goals for the next week.

Once the groundwork has been set, the mentorship will commence, and this will begin with the mentee providing some direction about the partnership. This could be a project idea, with an overarching question or hypothesis, for competition mentoring; or the key focus for an academic mentorship, be that a goal focus for each subject, troubleshooting one subject, working on one's social and emotional well-being, focusing on organisation, or something else. This direction enables the mentee to have some ownership of the mentorship and establishes them as being in the centre of the partnership.

With the direction of the mentorship established, the first set of goals will be agreed on and the mentee will be on their way in terms of their participation and action. At the next mentor session, which usually takes place a week later, a warm welcome from the mentor will start the session. This will be followed by a brief chat about life and how the mentee is travelling generally. A discussion around the progress of the goals (formative discussion) will then take place, before a new set of goals for the week ahead is agreed. It should be noted that the progress discussion, which is largely formative, will heavily influence the new goals, and sometimes the same goals might be set two weeks in a row. Sometimes the goals will be made easier if the previous goals were too difficult to attain, and sometimes they will be made more challenging if the previous goals were too simple. Sometimes also, a completely new direction might be required, and the new goals will reflect this. It is important for the mentor to be flexible with every new mentor session and to change the direction of the partnership in the best interests of the mentee. This is differentiation at work.

Key goals of coaching

As was stated earlier, I am a trained coach, having completed the senior growth coaching course with Growth Coaching International. Coaching has a very different focus to mentoring, because coaching is much more participatory in approach during sessions. The GROWTH acronym really guides all coaching sessions, but the onus is largely on equipping the coachee to solve their own problems.

Coaching is all about the coach asking the right question at the right time, and the coachee is required to come up with the answers and hopefully a clear way forward in the situation. Coaching could address any situation, and often coaching is used to solve difficult social or team-related problems.

The GROWTH acronym requires the coach to be responsive to the coachee within the given context. As a starting point the following outline provides an idea of how it works:

- **G** is for GOAL – What do you need to achieve? Tell me more about that.
- **R** is for REALITY – What is happening now?
- **O** is for OPTIONS – What could you do?
- **W** is for WILL – What will you do?
- **T** is for TACTICS – How and when will you do it?
- **H** is for HABITS – How will you sustain your success?

(ACRONYM COURTESY OF GROWTH COACHING INTERNATIONAL.)

The growth coaching acronym provides good guidance and direction to the coach in coaching discussions, and the training provides the opportunity for the coach to work through a range of scenarios using a much fuller "Tool Kit" provided by Growth Coaching International under each part of the acronym. Once trained, the coach should feel empowered to support a coachee in most circumstances, understanding that the coach is always working to equip the coachee with the skills required to empower them to solve their own problems.

Case study 1: When mentoring turns into coaching

Phoebe was a student of high potential nominated for the Year 12 gifted and high-ability mentoring program at the school where I was working. Phoebe was described by staff as having excellent thinking and reasoning skills, yet she had been performing below expectations in terms of grades. According to teachers who worked with Phoebe, there had been some issues with general organisation and prioritisation of set tasks. There had also been some uncertainty regarding how she best learned large volumes of concept material and subject content.

After establishing the above context with Phoebe as had been shared by her teachers, I discussed some possible options for our mentoring partnership moving ahead. Initially she wanted to get a feel for the mentoring process, so we started by checking her performance data and then setting some goals for her that might enable her to improve her grades. Goals were set and her progress was checked each week. This went on for four mentor sessions over five or six weeks.

Upon review of Phoebe's progress in mentor sessions 5 and 6, I found it strange that little if any visible progress was being made, when on paper most of her goals had been explicitly set, giving her clear direction for the week ahead. Historically, with most students, the set goals prompted some grade improvement as assessment feedback was specifically addressed within the set goals. Phoebe's grades were consistently in the 70% range, and though she was engaging with the mentoring process, in a sense she was just going through the motions.

As Phoebe's mentor, I decided to review the survey she had completed for me at the beginning of the year. This survey had some preliminary information about her school history, her passions and interests, her main goal at school for the year ahead, her main goal outside school for the year ahead, and her preferred ways of learning. Everything on the survey had been answered by Phoebe, so all answers were in her opinion only. No additional input was provided from teachers or parents.

Having reviewed her completed survey and her progress, I asked myself how I might set up a mentoring program to achieve best outcomes for Phoebe.

I wanted her to own the sessions and to own her progress and learning, so I started by highlighting the observed strengths that Phoebe possessed, not just according to me, but according to several teachers who had worked with her. Our discussion unfolded as follows, with me as her mentor asking her questions to promote her thinking and drive her actions. The headings are included to signpost the structure of the discussions, actions and the progress that took place:

Student ownership

Mentor: You have demonstrated to your teachers your higher-order thinking and reasoning skills, as seen in class discussions and collaborative group situations. Your capacity is significant, but your grades sometimes don't match your capacity. Do you know why?

Mentee: I am not well planned or organised.

Goal one discussion, including progress review

Mentor questions	Mentee responses
How do you plan and organise?	I diarise due dates then just complete the task.
What is your plan for each task?	My main objective is to complete it by the due date.
What structure do you use to complete an essay?	I just write from the start to the finish from memory.
Do you address criteria?	Not specifically, I just note what the teacher says is important and list what is important in no particular order.
Are you disappointed by your results?	Yes, but my priority is to finish on time.
Are you open to exploring a plan for your essays that you can construct and follow to see if your results improve?	Yes, but it will have to work for me to be convinced.
Would you also be open to looking at your key priorities in order of importance to determine your best priorities above just finishing everything on time?	Yes, but I will have to see the value in it.

Discussion followed of effective generic essay plans that addressed the key success criteria and best captured Phoebe's writing capacity. Phoebe created a written essay plan and showed me how it worked and how it addressed the success criteria of the task. The essay plan was then applied to the task with greatly improved results. New essay plans were written by Phoebe for each new essay, with each essay taking on board the key success criteria of the task.

Results: In subsequent mentoring sessions, we discussed the essay plans, and Phoebe highlighted how they were benefiting her preparations and clarity of thought within the themes. Over the next three or four essays, Phoebe's results saw an improved grade average of about 20% per essay.

As I examined the improved essay results, the way that the planning had unfolded during our mentor sessions, and the specific questions that had been asked, I realised that almost subconsciously the GROWTH coaching acronym had been applied, and I had moved from being a mentor to being a coach. This had been necessary in this situation, as I needed Phoebe to take an independent and proactive stand in her essay planning and preparation.

The application of the GROWTH coaching took place as follows:

- **G is for GOAL** – *What did the coachee need to achieve? Tell me, your coach, more about that.* They needed to **develop a clear and effective approach to essay writing** but, as the coachee said, they would also need to see the benefits.

- **R is for REALITY** – *What was happening for the coachee in the essay-planning space?* They were focusing on completing the task on time as a priority, addressing just what the teacher said was important and not specifically addressing the success criteria.

- **O is for OPTIONS** – *What could the coachee do in the essay-planning space?* They could keep doing what they had been doing to date, for results that were not pleasing the coachee, or they could seek out some generic essay-planning proformas and consider the success criteria of the task more specifically.

- **W is for WILL** – *What did the coachee do?* They agreed to proactively seek out the generic essay planning proformas and apply them to the specific essays that the coachee was working on. In applying the plans, the coachee also addressed the specific success criteria within the task in the planning.

- **T is for TACTICS** – *How and when did the coachee do it?* The coachee tried a few different generic essay plans at the initial suggestion of the coach. Upon finding one that suited their approach, the coachee applied the plan to the essay tasks they were working on at the time. This was done on a trial basis at first. The coachee had to see over a few essays that it worked for them in their approach to essay writing.

- **H is for HABITS** – *How will the coachee sustain their success?* The coachee tried the generic essay plans for one essay at first, and then tried it for another. Upon teacher feedback and seeing the significant level of improvement, the coachee then applied the same level of essay planning to future essays. Driven by the success of the process, the coachee sustained the essay-planning approach for the year.

Upon seeing that I, as the mentor, had reverted my method to coaching, I kept our scheduled mentor sessions with Phoebe, but I turned my focus to intentional coaching, as this was what was required for this student to participate intentionally in her own problem-solving. Brain-based learning highlights active ways of learning compared with passive approaches. Phoebe had been responding passively to her learning situation, and it was important for her to become more active. Coaching prompted this proactive action. Being a Year 12 student, Phoebe needed to drive her strategic change in pursuit of academic improvement herself. As her coach, I needed to ask her the right questions at the right times, but she would then answer the questions and action the changes towards improvement. Subsequent sessions progressed as follows, as further action was needed on Phoebe's part.

In her final year of school, it was hoped that through this approach Phoebe would take more and more proactive action and responsibility.

Goal two discussion, including progress review

Additionally, Phoebe shared some ongoing challenges with executive functioning, including tiredness, a random approach to subject work, an addiction to phone time, and not allowing enough time to revise for tests. I asked about daily exercise, which she said was minimal, and healthy eating. My observation was that these were all issues for Phoebe. Given the coachee's work and study habits, I asked her to consider some daily priorities that could streamline her daily life approach. Phoebe believed that several organisational challenges could be improved via a commitment to change. She believed that this could streamline her readiness for the school day ahead, improving daily work/life efficiency. These priorities included a commitment to the following:

- 7½ hours' sleep per day
- List of daily tasks including any plans to complete
- Maximum 45 minutes of phone/gaming per day
- 45 minutes of study/revision per day
- 30 minutes of exercise
- Healthy eating and more timely meals.

Results: After four further mentor sessions, I observed a much greater focus on the part of Phoebe each day, with daily commitments completely accounted for rather than her working through random "scrambling", and in many cases doing too much of one thing and not enough of others. Phoebe also felt that her schedule was far more relaxed.

So how did Phobe achieve this using the GROWTH coaching framework?

- **G is for GOAL** – *What did the coachee need to achieve? Tell me more about that.* The coachee needed to **streamline their day to ensure they were keeping an achievable balance.** They complained of feeling out of control and being driven by random "scrambling" from start to finish.

- **R is for REALITY** – *What was happening for the coachee in reality?* The coachee was being driven by their phone, particularly gaming and social media, to the detriment of other important priorities, including sleep and exercise. This was a daily occurrence.

- **O is for OPTIONS** – *What could the coachee do?* They could continue with the random "scrambling" and bad habits, or they could take some proactive action with the support of their coach.

- **W is for WILL** – *What will the coachee do?* They agreed to consider and discuss a set of daily priorities that could improve their daily work and life habits.

- **T is for TACTICS** – *How and when will the coachee do it?* The coachee established a structured list of daily priorities to address each day, some with time allocations. They agreed to make this list a priority each day.

- **H is for HABITS** – *How will the coachee sustain their success?* After just a few weeks the coachee said that by sticking with the daily plan of priorities they were feeling much more organised and in control. This was a good feeling that was lowering stress levels and something that they wanted to maintain.

Goal three discussion, including progress review

As Phoebe's coach, I also observed a lack of clarity about her ways of learning and how she best addressed set tasks. Aside from essay planning, which was now making good progress and her general daily study and living schedule (executive functioning), which was now more streamlined, I was still unclear about Phoebe's approach when embarking on an assessment task or test. To address this, I asked Phoebe about her preferred ways of learning, as there was still some confusion around this. I wanted Phoebe to understand herself as a learner.

I also delved into Phoebe's learning style by checking her start-of-year survey, then asked the following questions:

Coach questions	Coachee responses
Do you best learn with your eyes, your ears, by doing hands-on tasks, or through reading?	Not sure; can't pinpoint one particular way.
How do you generate information and knowledge?	I read and think about things.
How do you process the things you read and think about?	The things I read and think about become visual images in my mind.
So, is it possible that you are a reader/researcher, and you use your eyes to learn?	Yes, I don't use hands or ears as much.
How do you prepare for tests and exams?	No set method. I read, review notes, and just try to remember.
What if you wrote down key information or drew what you see in a structure or an artistic way? Could this help you retain information better?	Not sure. I will try it for the next test.

Outcome of the visual representation for revision

Phoebe tried experimenting with visual representation and mind mapping of key information for the next test. She then learned this visual representation as she revised for the test. This visual representation enabled far better memory retention, and Phoebe was able to refer to the material she had learned more easily. Phoebe came out of the test supremely confident, as she had been able to retrieve all the information, facts and concepts that she had learned for the test. The result was a 20% improvement on any previous test.

Results: Phoebe then applied the same method using various mind mapping and visual representation techniques to apply what had been learned in other subjects and contexts. She consistently achieved a 20% (2-grade) improvement in results. Phoebe was so convinced by this learning approach that the visual representations and mind maps were hung up all around her house, and each was committed to memory for future revision and reference. This was an exceptional outcome for Phoebe.

How was Phoebe's style of learning established using the GROWTH coaching framework?

- **G is for GOAL** – *What did the coachee need to achieve? Tell me more about that.* The coachee needed **to develop a clear strategy to study for tests and assessments that enabled them to tap into their preferred learning style.**

- **R is for REALITY** – *What was happening to the coachee?* The coachee had no clear strategy for approaching test and assessment revision. They were simply re-reading and thinking about what they had been learning and taking some notes to commit facts and concepts to memory. This was enabling limited success.

- **O is for OPTIONS** – *What could the coachee do?* The coach asked some questions to encourage the coachee to think about how they best learn. The coachee could either continue revising as they had been doing, or they could explore some visual techniques that might enable greater retention of learned content and concepts.

- **W is for WILL** – *What did the coachee do?* They decided to try out some visual methods for displaying learned content. They used mind maps and concept maps to create visual summaries of key unit information.

- **T is for TACTICS** – *How and when did the coachee do it?* They used the mind maps and concept maps to prepare for one test initially. They found this was a great way of summarising unit content and concepts. They stuck their mind maps and concept maps for the unit to their wall at home for ongoing future reference. The coachee was amazed by their greatly improved test results.

- **H is for HABITS** – *How did the coachee sustain their success?* With each new assessment the coachee created a new visual representation revision tool to summarise the unit work. Each time they added this to the wall. They found that they were able to remember all parts of these visual representations and they were able to retrieve the key information for tests and assessments with ease.

Group discussions

In addition to the 1-to-1 mentor sessions held most weeks, collaborative Year 12 highly able mentor lunches were held each term. The Term 4 collaborative mentor lunch was held just before final exams. This involved all members of the highly able Year 12 mentoring group meeting together over a lunch provided by the mentor. Aside from having lunch together, this was a discussion about the year to date and all that had been learned from the mentoring program – the good, the not so good, and the challenging aspects.

The mentor meetings had been a significant ongoing commitment for mentees, but many shared the personal benefits that they had enjoyed, and for Phoebe, the subject of case study 1, the mentoring had been life-changing. Phoebe felt that she was approaching her final VCE exams with great assessment results behind her, but better still, with clear plans and comprehensive documentation (much of it visual) for the revision ahead. Therefore, she had excellent clarity about how each exam would be approached. Phoebe now had a high level of confidence regarding her final exams. This was in stark contrast to the beginning of the mentoring program, when she had been overshadowed with uncertainty and a lack of direction.

Reflection

After the final exams and following the announcement of results, mentees were followed up regarding their achievements and in particular their perception of how the mentoring program had assisted them. I wanted to know if the students believed the mentoring had contributed positively to their final results. Almost every mentee believed that the mentoring had been helpful, and some felt that the benefits had been perhaps underestimated by some. As Reisner et al.

(1990) found, in addition to promoting the mentee's self-esteem and confidence, the mentor was seen by many mentees to have had an enormous impact on academic performance, motivation and attitudes towards school.

Almost all students felt that they had achieved a higher Australian Tertiary Admission Rank (ATAR) due to the mentoring program. Phoebe had no doubt about this. Given all that she had learned in the mentoring program, she believed it had contributed at least 25 points to her ATAR. Phoebe was delighted with her results and said that this mentoring program had come not a minute too soon for her. She was highly complimentary about the program and what it had meant to her and her results in her final year of school.

Case study 1: Results and outcome

Phoebe had greatly improved her essay planning and had refined her daily study and work schedules (executive functioning). She had developed improved ways of learning using mind and concept mapping. Her average grades had shifted from 70% to 90%, which included her essay writing results. In the end, when all of her assessment was complete, Phoebe's overall result was 96% with an ATAR score of 96. This was beyond what Phoebe had felt she was capable of in the beginning. This result provided excellent tertiary and vocational opportunities for Phoebe moving ahead. This was a true success story of mentoring and coaching at work.

In reflecting on this case study and the earlier part of the chapter, we have gained an insight into the key elements of mentoring, while also seeing where at times it might be necessary for mentoring to turn into coaching. The difference between mentoring and coaching has been explored, with mentoring largely being directed by an older, wiser expert. We have seen that coaching is mostly a participatory partnership where problem-solving and action is addressed by the coachee in response to timely questions from a thoughtful coach, leading to more and more proactive student action. Additionally, we have observed the commonalities of both methods and their benefits. These include active listening, a desire for self-improvement, and a promotion of safe, honest dialogue aimed at advancing and building capacity. With the potential for such positive outcomes, these disciplines clearly offer many benefits.

Discussion questions

1. What did you know about coaching before reading this chapter?
2. How do mentoring and coaching differ?
3. What did you learn from the case study in this chapter?
4. How could coaching be used in your educational setting?

Where relevant, come up with two or three answers for each question.

Chapter 3

A process towards student agency

"If you can't see where you are going, ask someone who has been there before."

– J. Loren Norris

Teacher wisdom can play a significant role in the success of teaching and excellent mentoring. As leadership coach J. Loren Norris advises, we should always learn from those who have been there before, and once we have been there ourselves, we need to learn from the experience, acknowledge what took place, and understand that it can be good to share what we have learned with others. This is making a contribution.

As I work from my fishing cabin today, I am putting this advice into action. I have had this cabin for 18 months and I am new to this area. I love to fish, but I don't really know this coastline, and fishing here is hard. In the short time I have been coming here, I have caught only a few fish. My neighbours have lived here for 30 or 40 years. They too are keen fishers, and I have observed that they rarely come home from fishing trips empty-handed. As I head to the surf this afternoon, I will be meeting up with these neighbours and I will be delving into their experience and expertise. I will be asking about the best tides, the bait to use, and the tackle I will need, so that I too can catch fish like they do. They are wise old fishers who have spent many hours on the beach, and I am aware that I can learn a great deal from them. Through these interactions I will build my knowledge and skills on the wisdom of others more experienced in this place who are keen to help and support me. They are unconsciously mentoring me. In fact, my neighbours have now given me a nickname – "The Professor" – because I am so curious and ask so many questions. This is what we ultimately want to see in our students, this probing for knowledge in the pursuit of bettering ourselves.

This leads me to the transformational nature of mentoring described by Clasen and Clasen (2003) in examining content-based mentoring. A well-thought-out, highly relational, and well-documented mentor program, with clearly set goals and ongoing progress checks, works through a clearly defined process. The process becomes predictable in structure but is adjusted according to the mentee's progress check feedback and the communication of what they say they need next. The new goals strive to enable the mentee to advance confidently to the next stage of their work with suitable challenges ahead. The mentoring cycle in Figure 2 captures this predictable process.

This weekly progress-checking and goal-setting allows for individual differentiation of the highest order. It is targeted and specific, striving for high-level challenge and engagement. It builds a scaffold between mentor sessions while addressing the criteria of the task. The student still does all the work, but it enables a clear way forward in small, manageable chunks, and eventually a detailed quality task is completed. Initially, however, this rich engagement and learning only happens with the social and cognitive interaction between mentee and mentor. Perhaps we should explore that interaction in more detail and consider what we have learned from the past. Such reflection can help us to more fully understand the possible variables of mentoring for best outcomes and maximum mentee value and transformation in the future.

Figure 2: Mentoring cycle

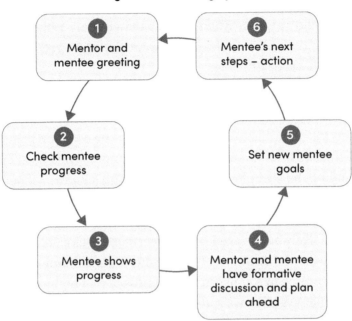

Vygotsky's social theory and the zone of proximal development

Lev Vygotsky (1896–1934), a well-known social development theorist, devised a social development theory which has significant value to us in this mentoring work. Although largely unknown until its publication in 1962, the theory "asserts that a child's cognitive development and learning ability can be guided and mediated by their social interactions". This provides exciting support for the mentor/mentee focus and intervention. It can be further explained through the three-ring diagram shown in Figure 3, overleaf.

In the inner circle, we see the challenges that a child confidently recognises that they can do themselves according to their current skills and abilities. The next circle represents what the child recognises that they can do with help, and only with help. This circle raises significant challenges for the child, who will be drawing on all of their skills and abilities, with help to achieve the challenge. This is a child's "zone of proximal development" as defined by Vygotsky and further explored by Eun (2019). It was briefly mentioned in Chapter 1. This zone is what we should strive for when setting mentee goals in the mentoring partnership. The outer circle shows what the child recognises they cannot yet do, even with help.

A mentor/mentee partnership working through specific challenging tasks demonstrates this social development theory in practice. It highlights the remarkable benefits of a mentoring program in helping a mentee to work through this developmental process in a most efficient way, building the scaffold of their learning with support. Once a child builds confidence and mastery within the ring of challenge they are working on, only then can they move on to the next one, when again support will likely be required. This aspect of the sociocultural theory is explored further by Scott et al. (2013), where it is building the learning scaffold according to a constructivist approach that highlights the type of process that Vygotsky was proposing when devising his theory.

Figure 3: Vygotsky's sociocultural theory of cognitive development

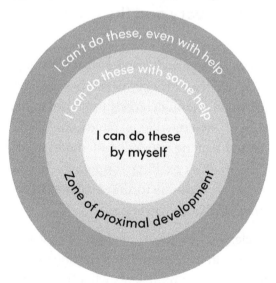

SOURCE: THE PSYCHOLOGY NOTES HEADQUARTERS (N.D.).

Supporting the social and organisational challenges for gifted students

Many students engage deeply with the learning process of a mentoring session. They value the relational nature of the mentoring discussion, which not only helps their social skills and skills of collaboration, but also enables them to reflect on their efforts, to organise themselves, and to ask questions that enable them to be guided clearly in their best move forward. As was highlighted in Chapter 1, gifted and high-ability learners need just as much support and intervention to thrive as do students with learning difficulties. In Chapter 1 it was also emphasised that often the greatest challenges for gifted and high-ability learners are related to their social skills, organisation and executive functioning. Again, here we see the significant benefits of the mentoring partnership in that it is social in nature, supporting a gifted student's social skills and providing social practice for the mentee at every session.

The mentoring partnership is also organisational in approach, with modelled progress-checking taking place in each session. It includes formative discussion of progress action, and a discussed plan of required next steps to inform future goals (see Figure 2, page 41) according to a student mentee's stage of readiness. This process is constantly setting up organisational action for the week ahead, providing an effective approach to a student mentee's organisation and executive functioning. Again, here we see a significant benefit of mentoring gifted and high-ability learners, namely, the direct action of addressing social and organisational development, two of the most significant areas of development and possible deficit for gifted and high-ability learners.

Emerging student agency and flow

Additionally, many student mentees will note the structure of the mentoring process, and once they have been involved in completing a few projects with the support of a mentor, many will ultimately transition to a position where they can work through the process themselves. This is student agency (Vaughn, 2020), which is viewed as a student's ability to own a task and become independent in completing it. As the mentee's confidence grows, so too does their ability and willingness to raise the task complexity and to investigate deeper levels of exploration. This is another example of transformational learning taking place (Clasen & Clasen, 2003).

During this deep level of exploration, students might become absorbed in their learning to the point of trance-like single-mindedness within their investigations. When this occurs, time stands still, and students will lose hours exploring the sheer wonderment of what they are discovering and what they are learning.

Case study 2: A trance-like state

In the second year of competition mentoring at my school, a mentee's parent approached me about an issue. Her son Ralph, who was in Year 5, was completing a maths project for the Maths Association on interest rates. Ralph was comparing fixed interest with compound interest and was applying this to his earnings now and into the future. He was exploring the difference in interest earnings based on the current interest rates and what he was investing now and what he was expecting to invest in the future. As a Year 5 student, his main source of income was his pocket money, but he knew that this would likely increase from Year 5 to the end of high school. Based on the weekly rate his older sister was earning, he was able to make some accurate predictions about future earnings from pocket money. Additionally, he was able to make predictions about earnings from part-time casual work as he grew older, again according to what was unfolding for his older sister.

Ralph was working with me as his mentor on the project, and he was exploring real-life maths and money within his proximal zone of development. He was asking investigative questions that he did not know the answers to, and he was totally engrossed in the investigative process of collecting data, completing calculations, analysing data, and recording the process and his key information. Ralph's mother said that he was not willing to leave the investigation alone. Every spare minute was spent on this work. When she asked him questions about his day or life in general, sometimes he would not answer, such was his level of focus. No sooner had he worked through one question or task than he would then want to move onto the next one, or another idea would come to him, and he would want to investigate that.

Ralph's mother was thrilled with her son's application to this work, but she was concerned about his all-consuming approach to the task and how it was impacting other areas of his life, including his ability to help around the house and his desire to work on the maths project rather than sleep.

As his mentor for this task, I explained to Ralph's mother that I believed her son was in a state of "flow" and there was a theory called "flow theory" created by Mihalyi Csikszentmihalyi in the 1970s that could explain it. I described the state as best I could, then I referred her to some Csikszentmihalyi resources which would give her a broader understanding of her son's state of mind. After Ralph's mother had read the resources, we had a further discussion, and she and I met with Ralph together to explain what we believed was happening and what he was experiencing with his work focus.

Ralph listened to us explain the "flow" experience, then he shared that he had never experienced this enjoyment in schoolwork before. He was loving the challenge and he felt like there was just more and more to learn. He described it as "a new learning adventure with every new question". Ralph could not wait to try out what he was discovering for real with his own money, to see if it really worked. He explained that the investigation was about life, and it was exciting. When he was doing the project, nothing else mattered to him. The doorbell could ring, and he said that he most likely would not even notice, and he probably would not answer the door. He explained that time whizzed by so fast when he was doing the project, but he was working through his goals, he knew what to do, and he was smashing it. Ralph could not wait to show what he was discovering to me, his mentor, from week to week, and although he was not thinking about the end of the project so much, he was confident that he could do well in the Maths Association competition.

We wanted to celebrate the deep level of academic focus he was enjoying, but we also wanted to enable Ralph to achieve some balance in his life so that he could complete all of the tasks that he needed to. These including general schoolwork, home chores, sporting commitments, family life and sleep. In the end, it was agreed that he would be allocated two hours a day to the project, ample time to complete it at a high level.

Ralph did complete the project. He earned a high distinction award and he was shortlisted for Maths Association nationals for his outstanding work.

Flow theory explained – Csikszentmihalyi

Croatian psychologist Mihalyi Csikszentmihalyi (1986) best explains this deep engagement experienced by Ralph in case study 2. Csikszentmihalyi proposed that "when one is actively engaged in an activity where the skills possessed are balanced to the challenge of the activity, s/he can approach an optimal state of experience called 'Flow'".

Csikszentmihalyi described eight characteristics of flow:

1. Complete concentration on the task.
2. Clarity of goals, reward in mind, and immediate feedback.
3. Transformation of time (speeding up/slowing down).
4. The experience is intrinsically rewarding.
5. Effortlessness and ease.
6. There is a balance between challenge and skills.
7. Actions and awareness are merged.
8. There is a feeling of control over the task.

One or more of the above characteristics will likely be captured in a well-set-up competition mentoring partnership, and at times all of the above characteristics might be displayed, as was seen in the previous case study. This is one of the very exciting outcomes of a well-designed and well-planned competition mentoring partnership, and once a student experiences "flow" they will not forget that level of engagement. Many will seek to work within that state to achieve their greatest learning enjoyment and best learning outcomes.

The project example in case study 2 was a deeply engaging and creative focus for Ralph, but it is just one example of an inquiry-based maths investigation. This leads us to a discussion of the importance of inquiry learning opportunities for gifted and high-ability learners.

The importance of inquiry learning and independent research

Inquiry learning is a strategy used to extend students' learning. According to Stonewater (2005), inquiry learning involves real-life problem-solving, deep thinking, planning, and teaching students how to learn, as well as what to learn.

Inquiry maths investigations come in many forms, and just about any focus or passion area could easily be turned into a maths investigation if it is truly measurable. So, if a student mentee can create a clear conjecture or hypothesis, if they can collect data, measure, record and analyse that data, and then make a judgement about the conjecture or hypothesis, based on the data as evidence, then likely the student has an inquiry maths investigation of merit. However, they must be passionate about the focus. Powers (2008) highlights student passion and interest as essential in motivating gifted and high-ability learners in independent inquiry.

In my experience, an overarching question set by the student works best to set up the conjecture or hypothesis. This is an open question which requires much more than a yes or no answer. It is an investigative question that the student needs to research to answer. I have then observed that a sequence of questions or tasks that follow the overarching question is helpful in assisting student mentees through the inquiry maths investigation process.

Below are just a few examples of some suitable overarching questions and their accompanying hypotheses that have been actioned by students completing maths investigations over the years of my mentoring work:

- **Overarching question:** Which state or territory of Australia is best at producing AFL players?

  Hypothesis: Victoria will be the best state or territory to produce AFL players because Victoria is the state where the AFL originated and therefore in Victoria many people want to play AFL.

- **Overarching question:** Which member of my family walks the most in a year and how far do they walk?

  Hypothesis: I predict that my dad will walk the most, as he works in the city and has to move a lot from place to place. He also plays sport. I think he will walk about 3000 kilometres a year.

- **Overarching question:** Which of our family pets costs the most to keep for 10 years?

  Hypothesis: Of our dog, cat, bird and fish, I believe our dog will cost the most to keep because it is the biggest animal and I think it eats the most.

Such questions, particularly when devised by the students themselves, promote ownership, engagement, and ongoing motivation for a student mentee to see the task through to completion. Such questions provide a level of challenge and necessary research if a student is to reach a conclusion and support or refute a hypothesis.

Further considerations for building student agency and high achievement

Inquiry investigations like the above examples will often excite students and engage them to the point of developing personal agency and striving for highest achievement, especially when the focus is in an area of high interest for the student. The task needs to inspire the student and drive them to work through the extreme complexities of the challenge. It is best for a student to have input into the selection of the chosen task. This way students will own their focus and be enthusiastic to work through the many challenges it will likely present.

When a student owns the task, it prompts their planning and design (Fredricks et al., 2010), and it motivates the questions they will ask, starting with their overarching question.

Understanding gifted, underachieving students

However, not all gifted students will find their proximal zone or work in "flow". As mentors, we need to recognise this and respond to students as they present in an effort to help them be their best selves in any presented task.

Siegle and McCoach (2005) identify four key reasons for gifted student underachievement and a consequent lack of motivation:

1. A cognitive, social-emotional, or physical issue.
2. A mismatch of the student with their learning environment.
3. Negative self-perception on the part of the student.
4. Lack of self-regulation and study skills.

I briefly touch on underachievement here because, as was shared in Chapter 1, underachievement was what got me started on this path in the first place, with the poor results of the gifted and high-ability students in my school. Sometimes, despite a mentor's best effort in the mentor/mentee partnership, a student mentee might still underachieve. It is important to know why this is occurring, to see if it is also possibly motivation related and to then address it. Hence this digression.

In considering the researched reasons for underachievement and then reflecting on the role of a mentor in academic partnerships, the value of a well-planned mentor should be extremely clear. Not only can the mentor be a support to a gifted student with a learning disability by breaking down the task at hand, but the mentor can also set up an environment that is safe and nurturing for the mentee. In doing this, the mentor is also building up the self-confidence and self-perception of the mentee through their optimism and belief in the mentee. Through this support, the mentor is helping the mentee to self-regulate, engage with the task, and work through a well-planned study process. A mentor has so much to offer any underachieving gifted student.

In addressing the question of what might motivate an individual to complete a given task, Siegle and McCoach (2005) propose two basic reasons:

1. Gifted students will engage with the task if they enjoy it.
2. They will apply effort and work to complete a task if they value the outcome and/or the end product.

This again is where a mentor can be of paramount importance – for example, when working through an enjoyable investigative inquiry project for the purpose of submission to the Maths Association for possible rewards and therefore clear recognition of student effort.

Embedding student agency and achievement in a mentor session

As we have seen, Siegle and McCoach (2005) raise some important potential issues regarding gifted underachievement and motivation, and they explain why and how these issues might be addressed. Keeping these ideas in mind, and the aforementioned theories of Vygotsky and Csikszentmihalyi, including how social theory, proximal zones and "flow" can impact gifted and highly able learners, we are well on the way to developing a framework of exceptional understanding for that first mentorship session. When a mentor has all of these understandings about a mentee and their possible needs, we raise the possibilities to another level for students. We make it possible to embed student agency and achievement that can be profound and life changing. When and if the need arises, the mentor should discuss these understandings and their complexities with the mentee so that they too can learn about these ideas and supports. This should happen naturally within the mentorship interaction, in which the baton of knowledge is passed on to the mentee as part of their self-actualisation process.

As part of their training, the mentor knows to support the mentee "no matter what". They know that they need to be that always-optimistic presence in the partnership, and that as a mentor they will continue to believe in the mentee. The mentor will model this positive approach to the mentee during every session, perhaps in part with the hope that one day the mentee might be that same positive and optimistic presence for someone else younger and less knowledgeable than them at another stage of their development.

The mentor will continue to check the progress of the mentee at each session. They will formatively advise the mentee on their progress, and they will continue to work with the mentee to set the most suitable goals. These discussions will take place at every mentor session, and at the end of the mentor session the mentee will always know what they are required to do by way of next steps and actions. This will be conveyed to the mentee in verbal and written form. The consistency of this process – which is predictable, reliable and clearly communicated – will be a constant source of guidance for the mentee, and each time the mentee is mentored the structure will largely be the same (see the mentoring cycle in Figure 2, page 41). In fact, through this cycle, it is hoped that the mentee will always know what to expect in terms of the method of the mentor sessions. The only thing that will change is the content of the session, including the focus and what is learned.

This process is very deliberate in that it is teaching a structural process of how to complete such inquiry projects using, in effect, a type of gradual release of responsibility (GRR) approach. First devised by Pearson et al. (1983), this is where, with more time and teaching, more and more responsibility for the task is passed from teacher to student.

Initially the mentor does a lot in terms of the mentor session and how it unfolds, but as time goes by the mentee takes more responsibility for directing the mentor session, and at the end of the project the mentee largely leads the final mentor session. In taking this responsibility, the mentee will share what they did to complete the project. This will start from their initial idea, leading to the overarching question and how the project was created. It will include the data collection, the findings, the implications, and whether the conjecture or hypothesis was supported, refuted or found inconclusive. This is the GRR in action. Let me highlight, we are just talking about the mentor sessions here, and how they run, and the purpose of the mentoring cycle as a guided learning tool. We are not talking about what happens between mentor sessions, because that is all the work of the mentee.

The ultimate mentor goal is to see ongoing high-level engagement, achievement and mentee ownership. Once the student mentee has completed two or three inquiry projects with the support of a mentor, it is hoped that the mentee understands the mentoring process so well that they are able to replicate it for themselves in any subject context. When a mentee can demonstrate this complete process with confidence, they are displaying agency (Vaughn, 2020). They not only know what to learn, but they also know how to learn (Stonewater, 2005), and they can empower themselves in this process to a high level of achievement, transforming their personal learning experience for themselves in all tasks.

Discussion questions

1. What is your understanding of student agency?
2. How can mentoring support students to become agents of their own learning?
3. Questioning skills are important. What makes a great overarching question?
4. Create a great overarching question. What makes your question motivating and engaging for a student?

Where relevant, come up with two or three answers for each question.

Chapter 4

Transference: the many facets of mentorship

"The key to becoming a good mentor is to help people become more of who they already are, not to make them more like you."
– Suze Orman

The key objective of a mentor is to guide their mentee through a process, allowing full engagement, creative expression, and in-depth learning on the path to a better destination. Many questions are asked initially by the mentor, and there are regular changes of direction as the objective ebbs and flows according to the new discoveries of the mentee. This is differentiated research which is responsive to new learnings and needs. This differentiated research might also lead to further questions as the mentee works to find more answers as they refine and continue their learning journey.

Well-known country music star and actor Jimmy Dean once said: "I can't change the direction of the wind, but I can adjust my sails to always reach my destination." This is the very essence of differentiation, where the approach or method of learning is adjusted to meet the needs of individual students. It is this shared experience and personalised adjustment between mentor and mentee that is so important in the transference of knowledge and skills from one party to another. It is this shared experience that sets up an environment where momentum can build, progress can thrive, and new understandings are passed on.

Transference: from mentor to mentee

To continue with the sailing metaphor, the mentor helps the mentee to adjust the sails using the mentor's learned wisdom and expert guidance attained through their vast experience over time. This adjustment is critical to keep the mentee on track while they dive deep into self-discovery. The mentor, like the captain on a ship, upholds the bigger picture, keeping the mentee's destination in mind, at least in those early explorations, until the mentee has attained enough knowledge to complete the exploration independently.

Under the mentor's expert guidance, the mentee almost always arrives at a satisfying destination in terms of product, but each time the mentee is experiencing a process structure of safe passage provided by the mentor. This process structure reassures and builds confidence for the mentee when the voyage becomes rough or stormy, and when the mentee might otherwise seek an easier route.

All the while the mentor is being a role model and setting an example for the mentee to follow. With each new mentor session, this process structure is again reinforced (see Figure 2, page 41), and as the mentee succeeds, they build confidence in the process, getting better at adjusting those sails for themselves and reaching the best destinations on their own. As the mentee becomes proficient in knowledge finding, and skill development, the transference of such attributes from mentor to mentee becomes evident.

The importance of content, process, product and environment – the maker model

Maker and Neilson (1995) share a wonderful model for practitioners and mentors to apply in supporting students to complete rich tasks. First devised in 1982, the Maker model, as it is known, is simple in structure, yet it drills down into the key attributes of purposeful differentiation, allowing students to keep it simple or make it extremely complex, depending on their stage of development. Its structure is perfect for inquiry tasks and hence is excellent for inquiry-based mentoring. The model is guided by four key words: **content**, **process**, **product** and **environment.**

Allow me to provide a picture of how the Maker model can work in this mentoring context.

In most new explorations the mentee does not know their destination. Initially they must trust that they will get there via a task design with sequenced questions or steps (content), through an efficient mentoring approach with goal-setting, progress-checking and regular differentiation (process), and a pleasing final project which has addressed all criteria (product). As the mentorship is set up, the approach needs to be highly accommodating and supportive (environment).

Maker's model of differentiation provides these four elements as a simple guide to such tasks. In later chapters of this book, we will look in some additional detail at content, process and product within the practical mentoring context, but in this chapter, we are examining the transferability of mentoring: from mentor to mentee, and from subject context to subject context. Therefore, the current focus is more about how mentoring can enable the right environment for this transference.

In establishing this setting, we are striving to create an environment where student mentees feel engaged, motivated and safe – a place where they can do their best thinking and have their eyes opened to Sternberg's (2020) transformational processes, which they will likely hold for life. So, as you are reading this chapter, think about conducive learning environments and how we can best foster these for our students. Let us start with capturing gifted creativity and task commitment as part of setting the right environment. This should allow quality transference from mentor to mentee, supporting the mentee to thrive in the process.

Capturing creativity and task commitment while developing gifted skills and knowledge

Creativity is one's ability to imagine or generate original ideas – the ability to create something new or to be inventive. The ability to create varies from person to person and is unique.

In a paper by Hennessy (2005), student motivation and classroom climate (environment) were found to be essential factors in maximising gifted student creativity. Before individual creativity would emerge and be expressed as gifted behaviour, students needed to be engaged in a process. They needed to be motivated by a task, and they needed to be empowered to pursue the task. Like Renzulli's (1986) three-ringed conceptions of giftedness (see Figure 4), gifted behaviour and outcomes were only achieved when above-average intelligence, task commitment and creativity intersected.

Figure 4: Renzulli's three-ringed conceptions of giftedness (first devised 1978)

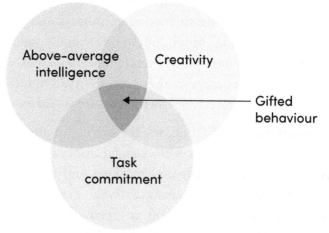

SOURCE: RENZULLI (1986).

So how do we enable this three-way intersection to be achieved, capturing high levels of creativity, rigorous task commitment, and gifted behaviour in terms of end products?

A gifted student will come to all tasks with above-average intelligence, but unless motivation is present, true intelligence will likely remain dormant and underachievement or mediocrity will ensue. This is where the mentor and the mentoring process can play such a critical role. The 1-to-1 nature of mentoring allows us to drill down into a student's task commitment. This is enabled through exploration of motivating tasks, by developing suitable research questions to explore such tasks, then, with the support of the mentor, setting up organised and incremental sequences to work through such tasks.

The mentor can provide the climate needed for students and the motivation to kick-start the process. The mentor can enable the discussion that creates the links to provide a clear, achievable pathway. For students, this is often the missing part of the jigsaw: the "how?" at the beginning. How will the mentee do it? The "how?" can be the blocker of task commitment and creativity, with a consequent shortfall in expressing gifted behaviour.

This "how?" is constantly reinforced when the mentor starts each new mentor session, revisiting the mentoring cycle as per Figure 2 (page 41).

Following an initial greeting at the start of the cycle, the mentor will commence the mentoring session by revisiting the individual mentee's project focus, exploring their progress, and determining their task commitment as demonstrated since the last session. The mentor will encourage a broadening of the mentee's creativity during the formative discussion, while looking at the plan ahead as new goals are set. Each mentor session will explore the unique attributes of the mentee and their focus. In this way the mentee can demonstrate their true individual and unique gifts through the work they complete as part of their talent development journey. As captured by the quote at the beginning of this chapter, the mentor is supporting the mentee to become more of who they already are as a creative individual. They are assisting them to maximise their creativity through sustained task commitment demonstrating gifted behaviour supporting talent development. This is all enabled in a safe, supportive environment where the mentee's self-expression is encouraged and risk taking is applauded.

This is transference in practice, and it can take place quite seamlessly in mentoring interactions where the environmental conditions are stimulating and supportive. As time continues in this space, the mentee will likely become more and more proficient as their skills and knowledge grow and as they discover how to learn as well as what to learn. In some cases, this growth will be so significant that the mentee may exceed the skills and knowledge of the mentor. Such transference demonstrates excellent mentoring as it is intended.

As we explore this further, let me share another practical example of transference through mentoring, this time observing a professional staff context.

Case study 3: Jade's developmental journey

I have a colleague who has given me permission to share her developmental journey. For this anecdote, let me call her Jade. In a previous period of my professional life, I had the opportunity to employ Jade for a teaching position in the school where I was working. Jade is considerably younger than me, but our values and educational philosophy are very similar, which led to a unified and common understanding on a lot of professional levels.

From the commencement of Jade's new generalist secondary teaching position, she was highly skilled and passionate about her role. She demonstrated the ability to promote an excellent classroom environment and she would always go above and beyond to create outstanding opportunities for students, sometimes with very limited resources.

Jade cared about every child in her classroom, and she would assist each student through a range of problem-solving techniques both academically and socially, in order for students to achieve their best outcomes and grow personally. Jade was a programming risk taker who would try new things in unfamiliar domains if she felt the students would benefit. She was extremely creative, highly intelligent, committed to the task, and very successful in her work.

In our early years of working together, I would sometimes discuss gifted education with Jade and highlight that, as a teacher who paid such attention to detail with individual students, she displayed many of the attributes needed for teaching students how to develop their unique talents. Jade was engaging in her classroom delivery, very inclusive with all students, excellent at differentiating her programs, and always pushing for maximum creativity and effort through purposeful tasks. Jade did not assume a ceiling of potential with students, as she always believed that students would surprise us, often going beyond what we believed they might be capable of. Consequently, she was always teaching up.

Over the years, we discussed gifted education more, and I would share my experiences of developing gifted programs in schools. Over time Jade became interested in giftedness and talent development and in time she had the opportunity to develop a gifted program in a school herself and to also complete some study in the field. She questioned me for ideas and resources, and she would read everything I sent her way. Jade was always seeking more information and ideas for new programs that might motivate and meet the needs of her gifted students. She very quickly learned that gifted and talented programs were unique and different in every school, and dependent on the needs of the students. Jade's gifted students very quickly became involved in public academic programs, and were soon demonstrating their gifted behaviour, excelling, and achieving acknowledgment and fame for their achievements, just as my students were doing. It soon became clear to me that I had been mentoring Jade.

This mentoring relationship has continued over the years as we have stayed in regular contact, and it has extended beyond teaching gifted students and developing great gifted programs or meeting at academic events or conferences. More recently it has been about working through relational dynamics with colleagues, navigating school politics, and working through the process of seeking new professional roles in schools. All has been discussed with utmost professionalism and always maintaining confidentialities.

As time has continued, I have also started to learn new things from Jade as she has delved into areas of gifted education where I have less expertise. She has also been a master of networking, knowing many more professionals than I know in the field, and she has secured some of the best positions in schools that have been available. Jade has excellent skills in information technology that have also enhanced how she promotes and builds her programs.

Consequently, what started out as a mentoring partnership, with a mentor and a mentee, has become equally beneficial to both parties, with me, the mentor, now gaining just as much from the partnership. In time I believe that Jade will supersede me in knowledge and skills, and likely surge ahead of me in the field. Some might say that she already has.

This is what mentorship is all about. This is how the mentor assists the mentee to fast-track their knowledge and skills, enabling them to achieve greater efficiency in a field more quickly, providing greater benefits to those they then teach or mentor and enabling the transference and subsequent transformation of future mentees. The earlier this transference can take place in a mentee, the sooner they will become proficient, and the sooner society will be able to benefit from their knowledge and skills.

Transference: from context to context

By now, you will be seeing just how transferable this mentoring process is. Not only is it transferable from mentor to mentee through skill and knowledge development, but it is also transferable by way of application to any subject challenge and almost any learning context.

One only has to reflect on the mentoring cycle shown in Figure 2 (page 41) to see the flexibility of its practical application and how it can very quickly and easily be learned as a process by a mentee.

The clear repetition of the cycle enables student mentees to commit it to memory and to refer to it in a range of other learning contexts. The task criteria are the other element that is critical to this cycle and part of the task design. Before a mentorship can be established, the criteria of the task need to be clear. These criteria will continue to drive the mentoring process, as success criteria are essential in guiding the parameters of any endeavour.

Initially I applied this cycle to an inquiry maths competition set by a Maths Association. Based on the cycle, I supported student mentees to set up 10 individual research projects, as discussed in Chapter 1. The criteria for this initial task can be seen in Figure 5 overleaf.

As each student mentee was supported through individual mentor sessions for their specific projects, they were also addressing each criterion from the "success criteria" listed in Figure 5. As the mentor, I was mindful to model the mentor cycle to the students while also ensuring that all criteria from the Maths Association project were addressed. No stone was left unturned in supporting the mentee through the project process as they commenced this new challenge.

From 10 student mentees in the first year, the Maths Association project saw 30 mentored students in the second year. Mentee success was very quickly evident from the outset, with almost every student winning an award for their individual projects in the first two years. As can be seen from the mentoring cycle and the "success criteria", students were provided with excellent support as they addressed their first true inquiry projects.

Following the success of the mentoring program in the first two years of the Maths Association project, it was decided to transfer the mentoring cycle to a Science Association project, a similar academic inquiry competition to the maths one, but this time in science. There were some fundamental differences in the Science Association project. These included the science project having a predetermined theme, whereas maths was free choice. The science project could also be presented in any one of eight presentation modes, but maths was largely presented as a book research project.

Figure 5: Maths "success criteria"

Tuesday 14 June

Re: Maths talent quest "success criteria"

Please remember the following important information:

Projects need to be complete and ready for collection by Mr Smith at 9.00 am on Tuesday 12 July. This is the first Tuesday in Term 3.

Whether completing your project presentation as a book, poster, model, etc., remember to show the full story of your project from start to finish.

Your project format should include the following steps:

1. **Project title** – Include your name and level next to this. (Don't list your school.)

2. **Mathematical aim** – This is your introduction, what your project is about, and what you wanted to find out.

3. **Observations, results and discussion** – This is your key questions written and answered in order showing all mathematical calculations, formulas or graphical information. (It is essential that your project flows and that you share the full story of your project).

4. **Conclusions** – What did you find out? Share some of your key findings. You could also make suggestions for future study on your topic (e.g., "If I was to do this project again I would ...").

5. **Acknowledgements** – Acknowledge those who have helped you along the way, but remember it is your work, not theirs. You can't say: "Thanks Mum and Dad for helping me to compile my statistics." If you say this, then it is partly Mum and Dad's work, not yours. Instead you might say: "Thanks Mum and Dad for your encouragement and support during the project process."

6. **References** – List the sources of your information (e.g., books used, websites used, etc.).

7. **Appendix** – Include this in a plastic pocket somewhere at the back of your project. This will contain all of your rough workings in dated order. Your topic form (summary) will probably be placed at the front of this. Include only your own personal work.

8. **Abstract** – This is a brief description of what you did and what you achieved. You should stick this on the back of your investigation under the heading "Abstract".

9. **Learning log** – This year it is compulsory to submit a separate learning journal or logbook of essential learnings, including

successes and problems that arose through the project process. This should include at least 10 entries, each a paragraph long with date or week headings. This must be completed as a separate book with the heading "Learning log".

Take pride in your presentation. If your writing is a bit untidy, type up the project. Do the best you can with your presentation and make sure your spelling and punctuation are as accurate as possible.

I am confident that your projects will be really competitive if you finish them off well.

Congratulations on your work to date. I am very excited about the possibilities of some really outstanding MTQ projects this year.

See you soon – Mr Smith

To keep a level of consistency for the mentoring cycle, I took the science handbook and adjusted the "success criteria" presentation structure, turning it to a format that aligned closely with the maths project while keeping the integrity of all key criteria. This was not hard to do, but it enabled consistency for students as they learned how to apply the new mentoring cycle to the task criteria.

In the first year of the Science Association project, I mentored 30 students. This was a new competition for the school. It was one that had been known to the school but had not been implemented. In the first year, applying the same mentoring cycle and the "success criteria" shown in Figure 6 below, the same mentoring process was addressed over eight weeks.

Figure 6: Science "success criteria"

Tuesday 22 March

Science talent search "success criteria"

Please remember the following important information:

Projects need to be complete and handed in to Mr Smith by 9.00 am on Thursday 21 April. This is week 2 in Term 2.

When completing your project, remember to show the full story of your project from start to finish.

Your project format should include the following steps:

1. **Project title** – Include your main project focus as your main heading with your name and year level smaller underneath. (Don't list your school.)

2. **Introduction** – Under the heading "Introduction", write a brief introduction on what your project is about and what you hope to teach the reader.

3. **Key questions** – With your questions as the headings, write and answer your key questions. Provide short, succinct answers covering key researched information. (It is essential that your project flows and that you share the full story of your project.)

4. **3 diagrams** – These need to compliment the research you have done through your key questions. Make sure each is hand drawn. Each must have a clear heading and each must be labelled.

5. **Conclusions** – Under the heading "Conclusion", share some of your key findings. You could also make suggestions for future study on your topic (e.g., "If I was to do this project again I would …").

6. **Acknowledgements** – Under the heading "Acknowledgements", acknowledge those who have helped you along the way, but remember it is your work, not theirs. You can't say: "Thanks Mum and Dad for helping me to put my poster together." If you say this, then it is partly Mum and Dad's work, not yours. Instead you might say: "Thanks Mum and Dad for your encouragement and support during the project process."

7. **References** – Under the heading "References", list the sources of your information (e.g., books used, websites used, etc.). Do this according to page 23 of the STS Criteria Handbook. This was handed out as a single A4 page.

8. **Finally** – Refer to the STS criteria page you were given at the start of the project process. Ensure you can tick every box on that sheet. This is essential.

Take pride in your presentation. If your writing is a bit untidy, type up the project. Do the best you can with your presentation and make sure your spelling and punctuation are as accurate as possible.

Stick everything to your poster wtih Blu Tack first to ensure it all fits. Only once you are happy with everything should you stick it down for the final time.

I am confident that your projects can be really competitive if you finish them off well.

Congratulations on your work to date. I am very excited about the possibilities of some really outstanding STS projects this year.

See you soon – Mr Smith

Again, success was instant, with 27 students winning science awards, including 18 individual bursaries, and the school won a major school award.

To those students who had been mentored for both competitions, the mentoring cycle (Figure 2, page 41) was already becoming familiar, and those participating students were beginning to understand how important it was to address "success criteria" in full.

As we reflected on the individual results of students in private, considering the strengths of the new approach, we also considered critically why in some instances awards were not achieved. In almost every case one of the criteria had not been addressed, or an area of final presentation had been neglected. This was helpful to student mentees and allowed each one to celebrate the many fine aspects of their projects, but to also consider where improvements could be made moving ahead.

Following the success of maths, then science, the mentoring cycle was then applied to "Screen It!", a movie making and animation competition. Again, the structure of the competition criteria were reconfigured, while maintaining criteria integrity, so that they aligned with what the student mentees were becoming accustomed to. Due to the complex nature of the movie making and animation inquiry, fewer students took part, and when it came to awards, there were fewer on offer. However, within two years, one of my mentees had won the primary animation section of this national "Screen It!" competition, and numerous students had been shortlisted and highly commended for their creativity and the attention to detail they had provided in addressing criteria and completing excellent movies or animations. The flexibility of the mentoring cycle was proving its value, and the quality of inquiry projects that student mentees were completing was exceeding expectations. The truly transferable nature of mentoring was enabling mentees to grow in confidence, and many of the student mentees were becoming autonomous learners as a result.

More importantly, the mentoring was enabling the mentees to become more of who they already were. It was enabling them to fast-track their knowledge and skills and to implement their personalities and creativity in disciplines they were passionate about. For many, this was happening much faster than had been anticipated. It was allowing students to engage more meaningfully with their learning and to advance their skills more quickly, not only in mentoring-related work but far more broadly across their classes. Students were more willing to try new things. They were taking risks in their learning because they were much clearer on the "how?" and if their initial efforts didn't turn out, they had another possible "how?" that they could try as an alternative. So, the benefits were becoming far reaching as the student mentees displayed their newfound skills beyond the mentoring sessions, transferring them into numerous classroom endeavours.

The next two chapters will look at two such mentoring contexts in more detail while exploring a range of examples of the mentoring process in practical terms.

Discussion questions

1. Define transference within the context of this chapter.
2. How does mentoring enable excellent transference of knowledge and skills within the examples of this chapter?
3. What personal attributes does a good mentor need for transference to be effective?
4. In addition to the mentor, what else is needed to support transference?

Where relevant, come up with two or three answers for each question.

Chapter 5

Competition mentoring

"My favourite mentor unleashed my passions, channelled my energy, guided my growth and encouraged my success."

– Anna Letitia Cook

In Chapter 1 I referred to a trial mentorship that I conducted with 10 students to address an underperformance issue with gifted and high-ability students in the school where I was working. It was my twelfth year of teaching, and at the time I was unaware of how life changing that trial mentorship would become.

The students in the school had been underperforming in an inquiry maths competition they had been entering for a few years. They had been starting their inquiries with great enthusiasm, working through the focus in their own time with some measured teacher support, referring to the Maths Association's guiding handouts, then by the due date they had been submitting their projects.

Sadly, they had not been getting any significant recognition from the Maths Association, and they had not been winning any awards. They were capable kids with great skills and knowledge. What could be wrong?

As I talked to participating students about the competition process, it soon became clear that the students were becoming confused by their inquiries. To use another shipping metaphor, they were getting lost at sea. They were sailing into the ocean of research with great enthusiasm but with a very limited range of navigation tools.

Inquiry learning tasks have so much to offer by way of choice and student exploration. The students were great at coming up with creative ideas which they wanted to explore. Some even came up with questions that they wished to investigate, questions for which they desperately wanted to find answers. Some students had even diarised the key dates for the task, but without some guidance and direction the inquiry became lost and confused, and the students were unable to produce projects of quality.

I hypothesised: could a teacher mentor support a student inquiry, enabling guided steps from start to finish that provided safe passage for a rich and rewarding student investigation and a great final product as the destination?

I was hopeful that it could.

The Why, How and What of the things we do – Simon Sinek

Simon Sinek is an English-born American author and inspirational speaker. In 2009 he published his first book, *Start with Why: How Great Leaders Inspire Everyone to Take Action*, in which he unveiled the "golden circle" as shown in Figure 7 opposite. Although much of Sinek's work is directed at business, his ideas have value in education and in mentorship. Sinek (2009) proposed that before we embark on any task or voyage, we should firstly start within ourselves by asking "Why?"

It is not Sinek's intention that the Why would refer to making money or extrinsic reward. The Why is about one's inner purpose, belief or cause. Sinek believes that when our inner purpose, belief and cause drive our actions, what we produce is richer, more engaging, and better understood.

Sinek's How is much simpler, and this is where we become more outward, hence its position in the circle outside the Why. It is not about How what we do is better than what someone else does; How is about the actions we take when we bring our best selves to address our Why. It's about How we bring our Why to life.

Then there is the What. What will we do? What will we produce outwardly? We know What the What is, but the quality of one's outward What will be determined by comprehensively thinking through and understanding the Why and the How.

Figure 7: The "golden circle" by Simon Sinek

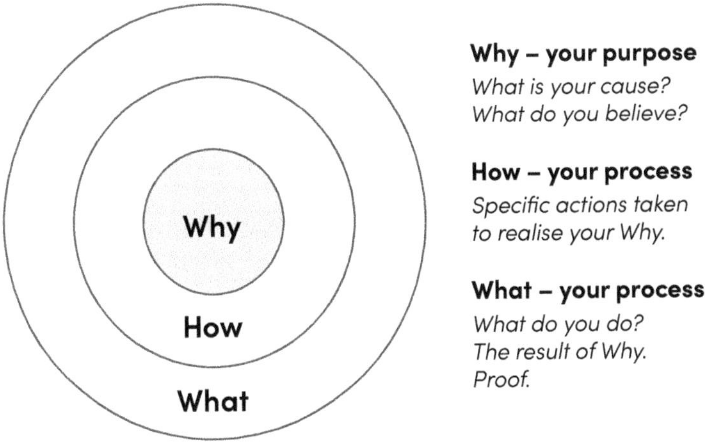

Why – your purpose
What is your cause?
What do you believe?

How – your process
Specific actions taken
to realise your Why.

What – your process
What do you do?
The result of Why.
Proof.

SOURCE: SINEK (2009).

Expert mentors serious about their task usually have a good grasp of this Why, How and What process when it comes to mentoring. Mentoring is a highly cognitive process which requires the mentor to look within from the outset, to use De Bono's (2017) blue hat, to think about their thinking metacognitively, and to have a clear idea of the task ahead for their mentee. Additionally, mentors do not mentor for lots of cash or external accolades. They are usually working away very quietly in the background, thinking step by step about how they can best support their mentee. First and foremost, they mentor to do a service and to support their mentee. So, from the outset their Why is reasonably clear.

In terms of the How, mentors draw on their vast wisdom and experience from years of practice. They call on the "success criteria" referred to in Figure 5 (page 62), to address the How with their mentee. And in regard to the What, well that is up to the mentee – the mentee will drive the What in terms of their final end products and What they do.

Mentees, on the other hand, are much newer at thinking through a golden circle type process. Initially, they fully rely on the mentor's guidance once an idea has been shared and a topic has been chosen. Having said this, for many of the students embarking on the Maths Association inquiry project, it was clear Why they had started it. When questioned, students usually said that curiosity was their starting point, not reward. It was nice to win a prize, but to start with they wanted to find out something new. When asked Why they had commenced with such enthusiasm, it was again usually pretty clear: curious students were up for a challenge.

As in Fredricks et al. (2010), these kids were motivated to discover something new for themselves in an area of interest and passion for them. In most cases, these students had topics of suitability and relevance, and they had a picture of what they wanted to achieve. Their Why was well placed and well founded, and many of them even had a vision for What they wanted their end product to look like, and what they hoped their end product might teach others.

In considering Sinek's golden circle, the issue for most student mentees appeared to reside in the How.

- How would they start this research task?
- What steps would they take?
- What process would they follow?

This was where the mentor appeared to enable a pathway forward guiding the student mentee through the How. Time would tell if that was indeed the case as I started this new mentoring trial in action.

The trial started with a teacher and student meeting where I presented a handout with possible ideas for a maths investigation. At the meeting I also presented students with a week-by-week timeline for the task, covering eight weeks in all, and a list of nine key success criteria that the students would need to address. The process for mentoring sessions was then explained to the students, and their consent to be involved was sought. From that first meeting the 10 students were asked to determine an idea for investigation and to come up with a broad or overarching question that could be explored. The question needed to be measurable using maths. Future meetings were called "mentor sessions" and took the following format:

Figure 8: Format of mentor sessions

Mentor session 1 (week 1): Finalise overarching question, set 5 additional questions or tasks in sequence for exploration. Goal: By week 2 investigate answers for questions/tasks 1 and 2. Bring answers to share with your mentor next week.

Mentor session 2 (week 2): Discuss progress and completion of questions/tasks 1 and 2. Make any changes as needed. Goal: By week 3 investigate answers to questions/tasks 3 and 4. Bring answers to share with your mentor next week.

Mentor session 3 (week 3): Discuss progress and completion of questions/tasks 3 and 4. Make any changes as needed. Goal: By week 4 investigate answers to questions/tasks 5 and 6. Bring answers to share with your mentor next week.

Mentor session 4 (week 4): Discuss progress and completion of questions/tasks 5 and 6. Make any changes as needed. Goal: By week 5 review all of your answers. Did you clearly answer your overarching question? Are any further adjustments needed to more clearly communicate your research? Bring answers to share with your mentor next week.

Mentor session 5 (week 5): Discuss progress and completion of the overarching question and any further required adjustment. Goal: By week 6 address the first 3 criteria from the list of 9. These are:

1. Your project title
2. The aim of your investigation explicitly shared
3. The maths tools that you used.

Bring work to share with your mentor next week.

Mentor session 6 (week 6): Discuss progress and completion of criteria 1, 2 and 3. Make any changes as needed. Goal: By week 7 address criteria 4, 5 and 6 from the list of 9. These are:

4. Your investigative questions answered and written
5. Your data clearly communicated
6. Your data analysis clearly communicated.

Bring work to share with your mentor next week.

Mentor session 7 (week 7): Discuss progress and completion of criteria 4, 5 and 6. Make any changes as needed. Goal: By week 8 address criteria 7, 8 and 9 from the list of 9. These are:

7. Your Conclusion – refer back to Aim
8. Your Acknowledgements
9. References.

Bring work to share with your mentor next week.

Mentor session 8 (week 8): Discuss progress and completion of criteria 7, 8 and 9. Make any changes as needed. Goal: Place everything in order into your plastic pocket book if you haven't already. Review the final book. Add any pictures or presentation enhancements. Are any further adjustments needed? If not, well done, great job. Put on display for the project expo and wait to hear if your project is selected to represent the school.

The outcome of the mentoring trial in contrast to previous efforts

After eight weeks of mentoring 10 students, I was astonished by the quality of what was produced. This had been a reasonable commitment on the part of the mentor, but the students had consumed their inquiry projects. Their passion and engagement was exciting, but what they had produced by way of rich inquiry research was exceptional. By breaking the task down over eight weeks with measured mentor support, the students had spent time in systematic research, data collection, data analysis, reflection and action. With the research behind them, mentees had solid statistical information and measurable evidence to inform their answer to the overarching question.

Additionally, each investigation was different and had been chosen by the individual student. There was a real buzz around what had been produced through this differentiated independent study (Powers, 2008), not only from the mentees, but from the mentor and other teachers who viewed the projects. The 10 projects were submitted to the Maths Association with confidence, and the results were impressive and well deserved: four high distinction awards (the highest level for the competition), four distinction awards (the second level for the competition), and two credit awards (the third level for the competition). Additionally, the school was awarded an outstanding school award by the Maths Association for being among the top five schools for quality entries.

Previously, in contrast, the school had not even won a single credit award.

Case study 4: An explicit example of a maths association inquiry project

This case study shares an example of how mentor support assisted one student in the Maths Association competition.

Billy was in Year 3 (eight years old). He was passionate about Australian rules football, which is played in the Australian Football League or AFL with an oval ball (in Australia we call the round-ball game soccer).

Billy had an AFL yearbook with lots of player data from the year before, and he wanted to answer a question about player data across the states and territories of Australia. Billy waded through the yearbook for important data and with the assistance of his mentor he used available information to set the sequence of tasks.

His first job, with mentor support, was to come up with an overarching question that he didn't know the answer to – a question that he wanted to research.

His overarching question became: Which state or territory is best at producing AFL players in Australia?

His hypothesis was: Victoria will be the best state or territory to produce AFL players because Victoria is the state where the AFL originated and therefore in Victoria many people want to play AFL.

Addressing the criteria for the task as set out by the Maths Association and as seen in Figure 5 (page 62), with mentor support, Billy set up a sequence of tasks. These tasks enabled him to address the overarching question from start to finish using extensive data collection, analysis, graphing and shared conclusions over eight weeks. As part of this process, the mentor met with Billy each week. During these meetings, the following tasks were considered:

- Determine the number of AFL players that came from each state or territory. Record this information in a data chart.

- For each state or territory, compare the number of AFL players produced against the total population for that state or territory. Divide the state or territory population by the number of players produced.

- Determine how many people per state or territory are needed to produce one AFL player. Record all of this information, including calculations, in your data chart.

- Rank each state or territory from best to worst at producing AFL players from your data.

- Graph your results accurately based on your statistical findings.

- Based on your statistical findings, which state or territory was best at producing AFL players?

- To improve your credibility for this research, complete the exact same statistical collection and analysis using the yearbook from the year before.

- Were your results from the year before the same as the original year? Explain.
- If not, combine the results for the two years of analysis to determine your answer to the overarching question.

The above shows the specific mentoring approach for Billy, but in considering such competition mentorships in general, the following eight steps provide an overview of the process:

1. Conduct mentee survey to determine the mentee's focus, which should be their choice.

2. Choose overarching question.

3. Create task or question sequence enabling the overarching question to be fully researched (see dot points above as an example).

4. Review criteria, which are provided by the competition body, in this case the Maths Association of Victoria, to set the parameters for the research (see Figure 5, page 62, for example).

5. Set weekly goals to break down the sequence of tasks for the mentee.

6. Implement progress checks, tracking work completed or not completed through a formative discussion.

7. Create new goals to support the student's next steps from week to week. Differentiation can take place at this time.

8. Evaluate the data collection, analysis, graphing and shared conclusions (see Figure 8, page 71, for example template).

The final body of work for this inquiry project was completed by Billy as a plastic pocketbook with criteria set as the headings and then all research completed under each heading very systematically. Billy added pictures and colour to enhance the presentation, which included data tables, data analysis, graphs, and mathematical conclusions from the data.

Finally, the project book was put on display with all the other inquiry projects at an inquiry expo before "Criteria Medals" were presented to all students who met the success criteria. This was done in acknowledgement of those students who had paid full attention to detail in the task. Finally, project selections were made for students who reached state selection.

Outcomes

The project in focus above – "Which state or territory is best at producing AFL players in Australia?" – was selected to represent the school at state level and was awarded a distinction award, which is a second level state award.

The above case study featuring Billy was chosen as just one example of a good inquiry project. Among other things, it shows the scope for differentiation within such inquiry projects – the scope for increasing complexity or simplification.

It should be noted that Billy decided not to complete the final three dot points listed on pages 74–75, as was his choice. Addressing the final three dot points would have increased the complexity of the project for Billy and would likely have led to him being awarded a high distinction.

Some other rich Maths Association inquiry project examples with hypotheses at other year levels

- **Year 3 overarching question:** How much would it cost to fill my family's pool with various brands of bottled water?

  Hypothesis: I predict that Evian water will cost the most to fill my pool, followed by Hepburn Springs, with Thankyou Water ranking third. Evian is a boutique water, and I think it will cost $3000 to fill my pool with it. Thankyou Water is cheaper, and community based. I think it will cost $1500 to fill my pool with Thankyou Water.

- **Year 6 overarching question:** How much pasta would I need lined up end to end to circumnavigate the earth, and how much would this cost?

  Hypothesis: I believe it will take 30,000 packets of 500 gram pasta spaghetti lined up end to end to circumnavigate the earth, and I believe it will cost about $45,000 to complete the task.

- **Year 8 overarching question:** In which country of the world would a person have the greatest land area to themselves?

  Hypothesis: Australia has a large land area and a smaller population, so I believe that Australia will provide the greatest land area per person of population worldwide.

What came next to consolidate the process

The following year 30 students were mentored for the Maths Association competition for 27 awards and again an outstanding school award.

Following the success of maths, as covered in Chapter 3, I was then asked to try the same mentoring approach for a Science Association inquiry competition with a similar format. Again, significant success followed at both individual student and school levels.

The same mentoring cycle was then applied to an information technology competition, and then a writing competition, with similar results. In fact, the school became known for the quality inquiry projects its students were able to produce.

However, best of all, through the mentoring approach, students were learning a process for How to learn as well as What to learn. The consistent and structured mentoring cycle was proving to be predictable and systematic for students. The mentoring cycle, with explicit mentor support, was addressing the How and enabling the development of student agency. In the years that followed, the mentoring program emerged as the greatest success of our gifted and talented program.

The mentor addresses the How for mentees

Referring to Figure 8 (page 71), we begin to see Sinek's How being addressed for mentees over eight staged sessions using a mentor. Let me explain in a little more detail how this unfolded for the mentee.

If instructed, many mentees will approach a first mentoring session with some investigative ideas and an imagined picture of what they might hope to achieve. Some of these mentees may even come with some possible research questions, but inevitably in that first session the discussion for the student reverts to How?

How do I proceed with the project from here? And for some mentees there is certainly a block at this point.

However, a well-prepared mentor assists the student mentee to proceed through the How as together they formalise the outline for the project via the overarching question, followed by the sequence of questions or tasks as shown in Figure 8.

This overarching question and sequence of tasks is the differentiated content that Maker (1995) refers to in the Maker model (content, process, product and environment). This content will be different for every mentee according to their chosen project. This content also provides the first step for Sinek's How for the mentee.

As the mentorship format continues, using the sequence of mentoring sessions in Figure 8, mentor session 1 sees the mentor encouraging the mentee to commence the true research by setting their first goal, which comprises the first two questions or tasks. Mentee action then follows via independent student research completed between mentor sessions 1 and 2.

Mentor session 2 commences with the mentor completing a progress check by asking the mentee about their progress, what they researched, what they learned, and what they achieved. As the mentee shares their progress, a formative discussion follows between mentor and mentee before the mentee starts to consider tasks 3 and 4, setting these as goals. These goals become the action focus of independent student research in the week ahead, leading to mentor session 3. The format continues as per Figure 8.

Subsequent mentor sessions are facilitated using the same mentoring cycle, as per Figure 2 (page 41).

Again, the mentoring cycle, modelled by the mentor, provides Sinek's How for the student, while also addressing the process of a differentiated task as described by Maker (1995). This process is systematic, consistent and simple, yet its application will work for any differentiated research topic when set up using a mentoring cycle with appropriate success criteria (Figure 5, page 62).

This takes us to the final submitted project revealed in mentor session 8 (Figure 8, page 72). This is the What that Sinek refers to, and the product in the Maker model. The mentee's submitted project will inevitably take care of itself when the Why and How of Sinek's golden circle, and the content and process of the Maker model, are well executed.

It is then critical for the final submitted project to be celebrated. One way of celebrating such projects is to share them more broadly, possibly through a project expo. Summative feedback by way of comments written and measured is also important and should be provided to the mentee in good time. Since the Maths Association focus is a competition with due dates, student mentees are provided with comprehensive feedback as a matter of course from a range of qualified experts, leading to rewarding closure for students.

This creative approach to a rich task executed via competition mentoring creates a dynamic educational opportunity for students, an opportunity that is different for every participating individual, and one that enables an optimal learning environment (Maker, 1995). Competition mentoring is not a simple process where we prepare a student for a one-off maths quiz or spelling bee (not that there is any harm in such competitions or support). Competition mentoring embraced through rich inquiry tasks is comprehensive, deep, and sustained over 8 to 10 weeks. It is transformational, providing a lived, standalone experience for students. Competition mentoring builds the learning scaffold and adds significant skill value for a student mentee's academic future. In this way, as put so eloquently by Anna Letitia Cook in the opening quote, the expert mentor supports the willing mentee in "unleashing their passion, channelling their energy, guiding their growth and encouraging their success" (Zhang, 2020). Really, what more could a mentee ask from a mentor?

So, what are my conclusions regarding the question: could a teacher mentor support a student inquiry, enabling guided steps from start to finish that provide safe passage for a rich and rewarding student investigation and a great final product?

From the 10 mentee projects completed during this trial, I think I respond to the question with a resounding "Yes", supported by the evidence that we see through the students' outstanding projects. This evidence is further bolstered by the ability of the student mentees to verbalise their investigations and their learning, the great pride that these students have in their work, and the new-found confidence that mentees discovered as they approached their next inquiry challenge.

Discussion questions

1. Why do you think that mentoring was so successful for mentees in the competition space?
2. Aside from how to win awards, what did mentees learn most from this mentorship experience?
3. How could such mentoring experiences build a child's navigation and learning toolbox?
4. Within your learning context at present, can you think of where students might be unclear on their How?

Where relevant, come up with two or three answers for each question.

Chapter 6

Mentoring for academic success

"A smooth sea never made a skilled sailor."

– Franklin D. Roosevelt

I think it is fair to say that the final year of school, Year 12, for any student is a somewhat turbulent one. There are regular assessment tasks to complete, ongoing tests, important exams, social interactions to work through with fellow students and teachers, and the sheer volume of work is significant. Students can struggle to find a work/life balance, they can battle to get enough sleep, and for some it is a year of constant peaks and troughs. For all students, including gifted and high-ability learners, it is a large undertaking that is rarely smooth.

However, school is about preparing students for life outside, so adversity needs to be part of this for it to be a realistic reflection of what will come later in the real world. Students need to learn to successfully navigate the rough seas that life will bring.

Mentoring gifted and highly able students in their final year of school

Having had success with mentoring in the inquiry competition space, and having seen the transferential scope of mentoring, I had the opportunity to apply the process, albeit somewhat differently, to the Year 12 context, initially with gifted and high-ability students. Understanding that all students are different, I did not assume for a moment that this Year 12 mentoring would work well for every student. To enable a best-match arrangement, I started with a screening process, working in cooperation with the Year 12 Co-ordinator and the Heads of House to provide a brief to students of what was involved and to seek buy-in from participants.

Some Year 12 students are highly independent in every regard, and part of the Year 12 challenge for them is to be able to show what they can do as autonomous learners. Such students, as academic all-rounders, have the skills and capacity to address their Year 12 year with full agency. After an initial discussion with these students, they were usually left to their own devices. Their data and well-being continued to be monitored throughout the year, and it was made known to them that they could seek assistance from a mentor if it was required at any time.

So, the students that I sought to assist were those with a challenge in some area: a relative weakness in a subject or two, some social and emotional challenges, or organisational issues. Only students who agreed to be involved in the mentoring program were included.

In Chapter 2 I shared a case study of a Year 12 highly able student with some of these challenges. In her case, mentoring turned to coaching, but in this chapter a classic Year 12 mentoring case study will be shared to provide a point of contrast. However, first let's look at the tools used to select these gifted and highly able Year 12 students and then at the setup for their mentoring, as well as some supporting research theory.

Selecting which gifted and highly able students would be mentored

Initially, gifted and highly able students made the priority Year 12 mentoring list based on their testing data. Every two years, students were diagnostically tested with the Academic Assessment Services (formerly Robert Allwell) test (2023), which included tests of potential covering general reasoning, verbal reasoning, and non-verbal reasoning. Additionally, students were tested academically in maths, reading, spelling and writing.

The test results were scaled as stanines, from 1 to 9, stanine 1 being extremely low, with students falling into the 1st to 4th percentile when compared to their same-age peers. These students required remedial assistance. In contrast, stanine 9 demonstrated an extremely high score, with students falling in the 97th to the 100th percentile for their age. Based on these test results, these students were considered to be highly able. The stanine and percentile correlations are shown in Figure 9 in a standard bell curve. Also shown is the intelligence rating from poor to superior. More information on standardised testing, bell curves, stanines and percentiles can be found in Gaertner (2022).

Figure 9: Stanine conversions to percentiles

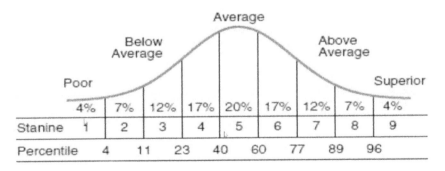

In addition to testing data, student grades were also considered for Year 12 mentoring selection. Student grades were measured in percentiles, and in the school where I was working, these grades were updated every day with each new student assessment, so a running record of progress for every student was available for viewing by the teaching staff and the individual child's parents. These grade results were a clear record of student achievement in every subject the student was engaged in. To be considered for the gifted and highly able Year 12 mentoring program, students were required to be within or close to the 90th percentile for each subject's grade.

The final measure for Year 12 mentoring selection was anecdotal teacher observation of practical student ability and talent. This measure became more and more important in the selection process. It included things like a student's participation in class discussions, the way they answered verbal questions, their ability in group work, and demonstrated leadership. In other words, it covered their demonstrated practical skills, showing what the student could do beyond testing.

So, at the end of Year 11, the three measures – testing, grades and anecdotal observations (two quantitative and one qualitative) – were triangulated to determine who should be included in the Year 12 gifted and highly able mentoring program.

The mentoring setup for these gifted and highly able students

Like the competition mentoring discussed in Chapter 5, I again agreed to support 10 students for a gifted and high-ability mentoring trial. I met with these students, the top 10 academics, over lunch (which I provided), and I explained what I proposed to do and how I believed it could be of benefit to them. My plan was as follows:

1. A mentor would meet each student for 15 minutes per week or as per the rotating cycle during the school term.
2. Around the middle week of each term, we would not have a mentor session but instead we would meet as a like-minded collective for lunch and group discussion.
3. The key focus of 1-to-1 sessions would be to support what the mentees were doing. The mentor would also be an optimistic presence in the lives of these mentees.

4. Each week, four or five goals would be set for the mentees. These might be subject goals, organisational goals, social/emotional support goals, or other goals, according to mentee needs.
5. Each week, or as per each mentoring cycle, the set goals would be reviewed, and new goals would be set.
6. As part of the mentor process, student data and results would be discussed.
7. Sessions would always be aimed at student support first and student growth second.
8. Students needed to agree to attend all sessions unless the mentor was otherwise informed.
9. Students needed to keep an open mind and see sessions as a time to consider their progress and reflect on all aspects of their course.

The 10 students agreed to take part, and following the first mentor group lunch, 1-to-1 mentor sessions commenced. Every 10 weeks or so, the mentor group had a cohort lunch funded by the school. This was an opportunity to review the program and get some honest feedback from the mentees. As I was working hard to be optimistic in all things regarding the mentoring, I asked the mentees wherever possible to be optimistic also, as well documented research from many sources tells us that a positive attitude goes a long way to bringing about positive change.

As shared in the 9-point plan for students above, the mentoring took on many forms. It was largely about developing subject goals for most students, but some students chose to work with the mentor to prioritise troubleshooting goals, others social and emotional goals, and some goals around supporting life balance. Students were generally very positive about the mentoring process, and most agreed that it provided an additional and important layer of support for them in their final year of school. Most concurred that it was very helpful to have someone in their corner backing them in their goals and life at school. The positive nature of the mentoring also gave the mentees greater self-belief and confidence that they could achieve more than they perhaps thought initially.

Supported by research and theory about best-practice learning

I was aware that a mentoring setup or process would only be as good as its tools of communication, and I knew that formative feedback would be critical in any such mentorship, but the beauty of the proposed program was its support from learning theory. In presenting their "five brilliant formative assessment strategies", as shown in Figure 10, Thompson and Wiliam (2007) show this all too well, and to further back the proposed mentoring program the school was adopting this very model of teaching and learning schoolwide.

Figure 10: Five brilliant formative assessment strategies

	Where the learner is going	Where the learner is	How to get there
Teacher	Clarifying, sharing and understanding learning intentions	Engineering effective discussions, tasks and activities that elicit evidence of learning	Providing feedback that moves learners forward
Peer		Activating students as learning resources for one another	
Learner		Activating students as owners of their own learning	

SOURCE: THOMPSON AND WILIAM (2007).

So, I was pleased to be able to share that all "five brilliant formative assessment strategies" as shown above were supported through a well-orchestrated mentor program, and a mentee who went through the mentor program from start to finish would consider **where they are going, where they are now, and how they will get there**, as per the top of Figure 10.

Additionally, I was aligning with the broader school focus, but to highlight this let me elaborate:

- **Clarifying, sharing and understanding learning intentions** – This was addressed from the outset, when the gifted and highly able mentees met for their very first cohort lunch. At that meeting the learning intentions of the mentoring program were shared and an emphasis was placed on the 10 gifted and high-ability Year 12 mentees being a cohort. The team nature of the group was emphasised, and the expectation that they would support each other and their broader Year 12 cohort was expressed. As a team, they were encouraged to set the academic tone for the school and to demonstrate leadership through this. Right from the beginning this told the participating stakeholders where they were going with this program, be they teachers, peers or learners.

- **Engineering effective discussions, tasks and activities that elicit evidence of learning** – This took place in every 1-to-1 mentor session as mentees reflected on their past efforts and set mentoring goals for the week ahead. Additionally, sometimes the gifted and highly able mentor group would initiate activities to support their broader cohort beyond the mentor group. Activities such as subject tutorials were the most common contributions. These interactions and initiatives highlighted where the learner was. They went beyond the teacher to impact peers and many learners.

- **Activating students as learning resources for one another** – This took place during the Year 12 gifted and highly able mentor lunch meetings, where much collaboration and discussion took place over shared mentoring experiences. In this context, students learned from one another and gained insights that they could take away, leading to richer experiences for themselves. Additionally, the subject tutorials that this cohort had been running for their broader peers in subjects of strength for them had enabled further learning resources. To highlight the inclusivity of the process, often students outside the gifted and highly able mentor group by invitation were also running tutorials. These tutorials ran in subjects of student strength and were attended by the highly able cohort. This was collaborative learning in action and highly beneficial for the academic culture. It impacted peers and learners and was valued by many teachers. It demonstrated where the learner was, and how they would progress further.

- **Activating students as owners of their own learning** – Again, there was some double-up in this active process. In every 1-to-1 mentor session, we saw mentees being owners of their own learning. Initially there was significant support from the mentor to assist with the setting of goals, but the student mentees did the work, and they were accountable for their actions from week to week. The case study below provides an example of such active ownership as we see the progression of student agency. These sessions impacted the learner more than anyone, but the teacher mentor was involved in a supporting role. This learner ownership highlighted where the learner was, and how they would progress further.

- **Providing feedback that moves learners forward** – This formative feedback on mentee progress provided by the teacher mentor in most 1-to-1 mentor sessions was invaluable to the mentee as they built their learning scaffold. Opportunities to broaden this formative feedback presented themselves at the Year 12 gifted and highly able lunches. Here the discussion was open, and the teacher mentor used the opportunity to share critical information in regard to things that were working well and things that might still need some further focus. This was largely delivered by the teacher mentor but it informed students and their peers and the mentee learners. It enabled the student mentees to see how they would progress further and how they would get there at the completion of their course.

Case study 5

This case study refers to Harold, a Year 12 mentee I supported in his final year of school.

I would describe Harold as a late bloomer, as his academic history had seen him building momentum in the last few years of his schooling. He was also a student who wanted to try everything and contribute to many facets of school life.

Interestingly, Harold did not qualify for the gifted and highly able Year 12 mentor group based on data. He was a very good student, but he was only ranked 27th of all the Year 12 students (200 approximately) based on his aptitude and achievements. Yet he was highly proactive. In fact, upon seeing that he had not been invited to join the gifted and high-ability mentor group, Harold approached me to ask if I would consider him. He did this via an email first, then a follow-up meeting at his initiation. It is hard to turn such students away, as with this type of diligence usually comes a strong and sustained work ethic – either that, or aptitude for high-level leadership. Either way, students like Harold usually make excellent mentees.

Surprisingly, I did not know Harold prior to his Year 12 year, but on closer inspection of his profile I could see that he had a wide range of interests and skills. Not only was Harold enrolled in a broad range of subjects, but he also studied two languages other than English and had a strong interest and an established history in community service work. Additionally, Harold had a high rating on his learning behaviours, which are rated by teachers twice a year to track students' subject effort and engagement. As well as a strong work ethic, I was confident that Harold was a person of character.

This character was clearly displayed at our first meeting as Harold delved into the mentoring process by asking me a range of questions before selling himself – and the contributions he would bring to this academic mentoring cohort – to me.

Following the meeting, I agreed to take him on. Harold attended the first mentor lunch and then we met 1-to-1 the following week.

Harold was a pleasure to work with. Not only was his work ethic excellent, but he knew what he wanted to achieve and the role he hoped I could play to support him. Unlike others, Harold wanted to set 8 to 10 goals per week. Most goals covered his subjects, but additional goals were set for well-being, physical health, and community action. His goals were each set as one-liners in the mentor book, or at least that was his intention, and once set he used his goals as reminders for his week.

Figure 11 is an example of his mentor book goals in a given week.

Figure 11: Example of mentor book weekly recording including mentee goals

Student's Name: Session 18 Date: 15 August
Progress:

_____ has completed all of his goals for the past week. He has received some positive assessment results for two SACs. Both were 90+%. SACs have been filed for future reference and revision. He has organised participants for the Movember fundraiser and has been sleeping 7.5 hours per night. He feels on top of things.

By 22 August:

1. Complete final revision questions for German assessment on 20 August.
2. Practise French oral in the mirror at home. Record on video for further critique and improvement. List three key improvements.
3. Work though Maths Methods linear functions tough questions. Focus on my applications in solutions. Complete eight by 18 August.
4. Seek written feedback from maths teacher on linear functions tough questions.
5. Finish homework by 10 pm each night, be in bed by 10.30 pm, and lights out by 11 pm.
6. Walk my 2 km stretch of the beach every second day or at least three times this week.
7. Add six key words and meanings to my English language glossary this week.
8. Complete one English language essay for teacher review this week. Focus on use of meta-language as per teacher feedback last time.

9. Complete eight cue cards with questions on the front and answers on the back for history this week.

10. Sign up five new people for Movember this week.

Complete the above and talk through my results with Mr Smith at the next mentor session on 22 August.

Please note: The above goals did not include Harold's subject homework each week. The above was all additional work – we called it the "one percenters" that would give a mentee an edge.

The above mentor notes were discussed reflectively at the mentor session on 22 August. During that time Harold showed me what had been completed, which for him was usually everything. We discussed what had worked well and what had been challenging, and those goals that were completed were ticked off. Harold then used this formative discussion to inform his new goals for the week ahead. Again, with mentor support he would complete about 10 goals and the mentoring cycle would continue. Again, see the mentoring cycle in Figure 2 (page 41).

Power of the formative discussion

Through this 1-to-1 mentoring process, we see the impact of Thompson and Wiliam's (2007) "five brilliant formative assessment strategies" in action. Although all five add significant value in the broader mentoring process for the gifted and highly able Year 12 cohort, as was shared earlier in this chapter, when it comes to the 1-to-1 focus the mentor is certainly:

*   Engineering effective discussions, tasks and activities that elicit evidence of learning for the mentee
*   Providing feedback that moves the student mentee forward, AND
*   Activating the student mentee to be an owner of their own learning. See Figure 10 (page 86).

These formative discussions between the mentor and the mentee help the mentee to see where they are up to in their learning and action progress. This empowers them to see how they can go further in exploring their self-efficacy, monitoring their self-regulation, and building their learning scaffold through purposeful action.

Power of reflection

Additionally, we see the mentor conveying the power of self-reflection to the mentee through formative discussions that ask the mentee to look at past efforts and learnings to inform not only the progress of the mentee so far but also their future goals and direction (Vrabie, 2021). During the busy Year 12 year, many students feel they have limited time to reflect on their work or progress. They are encouraged to reflect through formative teacher feedback on assessments, and some students do it better than others. Mentoring sessions provide another avenue for this reflection, which is critical for students in building their learning scaffold as they discuss their progress and set new goals.

Power of support and advocacy

The power of mentor support and advocacy cannot be underestimated. Nick (2012) discusses the impact of mentor advocacy used to build confidence and proficiency in a different professional field, yet mentor advocacy has the same impact regardless of the field. Mentor advocacy is like a backing or mentee endorsement; it is having a trusted older expert in your corner, taking watch, and supporting, encouraging and noticing your progress. In this case study, Harold gained much confidence from this knowledge and advocacy. Additionally, he was happy to ask for mentor advocacy with a subject teacher when he felt it could support him in a situation.

Outcomes

From a ranking of 27 in the cohort at the end of Year 11, Harold was the outright dux for his Year 12 cohort, scoring an Australian Tertiary Admission Rank (ATAR) of 99.9, just 0.05 shy of a perfect score. In assemblies and formal occasions following his result, Harold spoke glowingly of the Year 12 gifted and high-ability mentor program, not just from the perspective of his final result but also regarding the habits it helped him to establish and the invaluable discipline that it enabled him to develop. To his credit, Harold felt that a mentor would also be highly beneficial to him in his future study, work and life – and there ends this case study.

The results of mentoring these gifted and high-ability students

At the end of the first year of Year 12 mentoring, students performed well above their potential based on their initial stanine assessments. Many achieved in the top 1% of all Year 12 students across the state, and almost all finished in the top 5%. This was considered a great success by school senior management, given that the identified mentees had been in the top 10%, and some had only just fallen into that category based on assessments and grades.

As the Year 12 mentoring program continued, its reputation developed and school senior management asked me to take on more students. Within just three years, I was mentoring 20 gifted and highly able Year 12 students each year, and my full-time mentoring equivalent grew by a day a week. Harold from case study 5 above was a student in my third year as mentor of this program. As the years passed, aligning with the narrative of case study 5, and based on the historic results of past participants, students sought to gain a place in the program, and the results of mentees continued to be excellent.

Providing targeted mentor support to underachievers in their final year of school

This led to the need to address a new problem at this same school, where the bottom 20 Year 12 students were not performing well, were in some cases letting themselves down, and were impacting the school results by way of ranking. Management wanted to see this cohort at least represent themselves as well as they could, and mentoring was deemed a potential way of achieving this.

A mentoring program was set up within this cohort, which we called the targeted mentor group. Again, students had to provide consent to be involved, and they worked to address fewer, but similar, goals. Mentors were selected to support these students based on like-minded connections. These mentors were trained in the mentoring process, and they worked to meet students regularly. The mentors demonstrated great optimism as they supported these targeted mentees.

Selection of targeted mentees

Selecting the targeted mentees to be involved in the targeted mentor program was done similarly to the selection process for the gifted and highly able students shared earlier, but in reverse. The same diagnostic tests were drawn on and the same subject grade system was examined. Additionally, the same anecdotal observations by teachers were used, and teachers then provided recommendations, but this time we were looking at the most vulnerable students in Year 12 based on their Year 11 information.

In attempting to draw out the 20 most vulnerable students for this mentorship, we were looking at students who would likely be at high risk of not meeting the Year 12 certificate requirements for a passing grade. Some students who fell into this category were bypassed because they were receiving support from other programs. If a student was already receiving special needs support from the learning enhancement department, or special provision via another school channel, then we knew they were being supported and could be bypassed. Additionally, some of the most vulnerable students were receiving significant counsellor support for their social and emotional well-being. This social and emotional support was a priority for these students first and foremost, so some of these students were also bypassed for the Year 12 targeted mentor program.

Once all alternative support measures had been considered, the selection process looked at the lowest stanines in the diagnostic tests, the lowest grades in the subject assessment data, and anecdotal referrals from teachers. Again, student participation was viewed from the angle that this mentor support program had been designed to support students to be their best selves in their final year of school. The hope was that they might be in a position to represent themselves well academically. Only students who agreed took part.

Selection of targeted mentors

The selection of mentors for the targeted mentor group was based firstly on relational connections. Past experience had informed me that unless a good connection was made between mentor and mentee, and mentees were feeling that the mentoring **environment** (Maker 1995) was comfortable, students would not wish to engage. Additionally, these mentees would be ill equipped to complete their best work. In selecting the most suitable mentors, the individual mentees were each closely examined in terms of their needs and the most appropriate mentor match. Usually, male mentees met with a male mentor, and female mentees met with a female mentor, but this was not always possible. More important than gender was the like-mindedness and the academic alignment. So, if a mentee had a particular subject teacher match, a subject teacher might then become their mentor; or if a mentee identified with a specific sports coach, music coach or house tutor, that staff member might then become the mentor for that mentee.

Such matches were closely orchestrated, and there was process input from multiple staff who worked with the cohort to decide. These staff included the Year 12 coordinator, the head of school, house coordinators, and other key stakeholders. The mentor/mentee match was critical to the success of the mentorship, so careful thought, time and collaboration was given to the process. Once determined, both the mentor and the mentee had to agree on the partnership.

Setting goals for targeted mentor support

Below are some examples of the types of mentoring goals that I would set from week to week for students who needed additional support in the targeted mentor group. All goals would need to have a due date, usually the next mentoring session. Each goal needed to be reviewed when checking student progress. Student mentees were also encouraged with their mentor to reflect on their achievement of each goal. Goals were to be challenging, but realistic. Three or four goals were set, according to what the student mentee could manage at the time.

Goals supporting targeted mentees could usually be categorised under one of four categories:

1. Executive functioning/organisational
2. Trouble-shooting
3. Study skills
4. Social/emotional support.

I will now share some typical examples of goals for each:

1. **Executive functioning/organisational**

   - *English:* Re-write last week's essay submission addressing all of the teacher feedback provided. Align with task criteria and re-submit. Bring a copy to show me.

   - *History:* Complete history timeline and annual profile summaries for the years between 1842 and 1852 according to the task criteria provided.

   - *Biology:* Summarise Chapter 3, "Enzymes", by answering the study questions at the end of the chapter. For each paragraph of the chapter write a dot point statement that summarises its content.

2. **Trouble-shooting**

   - *English:* Before leaving school tomorrow, find Mr Glover and ask him to clarify the feedback he provided in the last essay. Ask him to provide three key instructions for your re-submission next week.

   - *History:* Given that your annual profile summaries (APS) for the years 1842 to 1852 lacked literary support, find a quote from your text or another suitable source that explains a key community or government focus each year at that time. Insert these into your new APS draft and reference correctly.

- *Biology:* Your biology test result would indicate sound understanding of Chapter 3 components, including 3.1, 3.2 and 3.4. However, 3.3 demonstrated a poor understanding. Read 3.3 again. Once read, summarise its contents in words. Draw three diagrams that highlight the contents of that part of the chapter and label each one. Redo the summary study questions for 3.3. Self-correct, ready to show me.

3. **Study skills**

- *English:* Review the essay you completed for Mr Glover. It is much better now it is aligned with the task criteria in full, and also now you have acted on Mr Glover's feedback. You are aware of the three key instructions that Mr Glover has referred to as essential and you have acted on them. Complete a final edit to see if you can improve your writing at all. Replace weak words with better words. Punctuate sentences according to the meaning and expression you wish to convey. Ensure you have answered the essay question in full and to the best of your ability. Make changes in red as required. Show me at the next mentoring session.

- *History:* Complete a visual mind map (A4 only) summarising your history timeline and annual student profile summaries. Try to include everything of importance within this focus for future reference. Be reasonably detailed.

- *Biology:* Write down 30 key questions that will assist you in summarising Chapter 3, "Enzymes". Write them onto cue cards with the question on one side and the correct answer on the back. Keep these as you formulate your cue card bank for all biology chapters this year. Use a different-coloured cue card for each biology chapter. This will differentiate the chapters. Keep for future study reference as required.

4. **Social/emotional support**

- *Sleep:* You are looking extremely tired. Ensure you are achieving at least 7 hours sleep a night. Keep a record of sleep per night. Share progress next week.

- *Health:* Your cough is getting worse. Please ensure you see the doctor as soon as possible before it gets any worse. Consider some Strepsils or Soothers and some warm tea before sleeping. Report back.

- *Eating:* Make sure you have your lunch during the lunch break each day. Your energy levels and performance will drop if you aren't disciplined with this. Keep a record of when lunch is eaten each day this week and report back.

In order to keep up with the best goals for the student mentee, it was necessary to ask the mentee a number of questions about their course and to get them to share details regarding their house mentor/coordinator, their subjects, their due date calendar, their teachers for each subject, and their timetable. There were times when mentors needed to communicate with teachers and parents about the student mentee.

The results of targeted mentor support

At the end of the first year of implementation, results were a stark contrast to previous years. Instead of having 10 students not meeting the requirements of the final year of school, this had now been reduced to just two or three, and the end scores of almost every student were significantly better than previous years.

Not only were most students achieving close to their best efforts and hence being afforded much better tertiary offerings or vocational prospects, but the school's VCE ranking shifted from close to 100 in the state, to a rank of 30, a result that has now been sustained for the last seven years.

Additionally, invaluable life skills were being taught to almost every targeted mentee around communication, planning, organisation and discipline. Some mentors believed that these skills were the most important benefit of the program for these students above and beyond an improved academic result. Communication, planning, organisation and discipline are skills that these students will carry and apply beyond school. Beyond any academic result, these are the skills that employers want and need, so above scores and statistics, mentors applauded the practical value of the program as well.

Being one's best self – working in proximal zones

In the end, all agreed that mentoring programs are about supporting a student's best efforts. They are about the aforementioned skill development, but they are also about plugging the deficits and negotiating the distractions that present as crags, rocks and rough seas along the journey. They are about enabling students to work to their capacity within their peak proximal zones (Eun 2019), and according to the timing of their development. More than that, the process of mentoring and the skills taught by the mentor enable the mentee to continue the journey with what they need to successfully tackle any future problem and to scaffold their skills to their own destinations. As Franklin D. Roosevelt said, "A smooth sea never did make a skilled sailor." The skills come from the challenges and the difficulties and how they are negotiated; these challenges and difficulties will continue to come, but when a mentee has the correct tools to navigate them and surge ahead, that is when they fill their sails in work and in life. That is when the mentee thrives, demonstrating their best self in their everyday decisions, actions and destinations. Ultimately, this is what we want for every student in every school, and it is reassuring to know that a mentor can go a long way towards making this developmental progression a reality for many mentees.

Discussion questions

1. What are the most critical elements of the mentoring process when it comes to successful academic mentoring?

2. What attributes did Harold have that we should aspire to with our students?

3. Explain how mentoring can assist students to develop desirable attributes that could support them for life?

4. Every educational setting is different, but how might academic mentoring work in your educational space? (Would any adjustments be needed? Explain.)

Where relevant, come up with two or three answers for each question.

Chapter 7

Authentic intentions and personal growth

"The heart of mentoring – Getting the most out of life isn't about how much you keep for yourself but how much you pour into others."
– David Stoddard

I do not claim to be the perfect role model. I have made my share of mistakes, and I have learned a great deal from them. I have regrets that run deep and at times still rise up to impact my well-being. These present as traumatic events of days gone by, some fleeting, some sustained. There were times when I could have managed my emotions better, times when I should have responded differently... but a renewing has come through specialist support and restorative justice.

In part, significant events have shaped my past, but mostly they have led to a more interesting future. I have not moved through life the way I expected, but who has?

The journey has been different, with many twists and turns, but it has still been richly rewarding, and I have been able to develop a stronger mindset, greater resilience, and gratitude for all that I have, and the outlook is bright. This is life as we live it. It is what makes us who we are – it's what makes us human.

Growing wisdom from life's lessons

As I look back on past choices, and resulting outcomes, I have come to understand that it is all about intentions. Did any decision come from a bad place, or was every action well intended?

Did the action arise to help someone, to advance a cause, to bring about positive change, to solve a problem, or to serve an important purpose? These types of questions need to drive our motives to ensure authentic intentions and the best possible outcomes.

Having said this, mistakes are part of life and learning, and to dwell on them is unhelpful. We must learn from the errors of our past, try to reduce their prevalence in the future, and move on with wisdom from hindsight. Usually, what we do next will be better and more measured because of what we learned from past mistakes.

This learned wisdom and the resulting refined beliefs are what mentors need to convey to their mentees in the mentoring process. It is this lived mentor experience and wisdom accumulated through years of living that brings so much value to the mentee. As actor, comedian and singer-songwriter Lily Tomlin once said: "The road to success is always under construction". How well this highlights the journeying path of a lifelong learner, be they mentor or mentee.

The learning journey ahead

With Lily's thoughts in mind, I can confidently say that I learn something new every day. These learnings come from students, my fishing neighbours mentioned in Chapter 1, my spouse, my own adult children, or a random person in the street. Every day I add something new to my list of learnings and I tuck it away for future reference, to help me on my road to success.

But it is not enough to just learn these new things. Hopefully, what I learn adds to my wisdom bank and enhances my personality and my ability to give back in a positive way. Hence, I hope that these new learnings can contribute to the greater good in society and be clearly shared through my words and actions. Hopefully, these new learnings will come through in my interactions with others and the way in which I set up mentorships and approach the value I can add to my mentees in various contexts.

I have learned some important things in recent decades about the mentoring journey and the most important considerations of that learning process. There are some things that work almost every time, and there are other things that are certain deal breakers. Let me share a few of the most important considerations for mentors.

1. Listening and the investment of time

A good mentor needs to be present in the moment and fully available to their mentee. It is possible for a person to be physically present but mentally absent. Indeed, I had a period of time in my life when this was the case. Under extreme stress professionally, all my attention was given to the professional problem I was working through, and nothing was being provided to those around me who needed my input. I was incapable of listening constructively to the family issues of the day and instead I became a distant figure, a shell in the room. I was present, but I wasn't.

During busy times with lots of competing priorities this is a risk for any mentor and any leader. Very quickly the potency of impact is lost, and it takes a concerted effort and time to win back the trust and rapport that went missing. Investing time and listening actively is about being fully present in the moment and being available to think, respond and support the issue to one's full capacity in that time and place. This is critical in good mentoring, and it goes a long way towards building a trusting relationship. Some say they can multitask. When mentoring, there is one task, and our attention needs to be undivided.

2. The power of Socratic questions

Great mentors become thoughtful questioners. It is a mentor's ability to question that enables them to get to know their mentee and to drill down into the issues at hand, be they academic or social and emotional. Questions also demonstrate a mentor's thoughts and interest in the focus, thus building rapport and investment with the mentee.

VanTassel-Baska (2023) highlights the importance of Socratic questioning with gifted learners, not necessarily in the mentoring context, but generally to extend a student's depth of knowledge and skills, and to build talent. Socratic questions are inquiry- and debate-type questions that look for logical, well-thought-out responses. They might be clarification questions, assumption questions or reason-and-evidence-type questions. They are often used to build complexity and depth within a focus.

Socratic questions promote interest and investment from both mentor and mentee, and they help to align the relationship and to get both parties on the same page. If a mentor is ever struggling to start the mentorship or build the conversation, they should first think of some great Socratic questions relevant to the task of focus. This will very quickly help with building the common connection and providing a direction for the mentorship.

Examples of Socratic questions to build momentum around a focus can be as simple as:

- Why do you say that?
- What do you mean by...?
- How does this relate to our discussion?
- What do you think is the main issue?
- Could you expand upon that point further?

Socratic questions are those that require a much deeper, more thoughtful response, above and beyond a yes or a no.

3. The power of recording and reviewing our reflections

I have always been an advocate for taking written notes in mentoring sessions. I might be old school, but I like to write down a record of the discussion, to pass a copy to the mentee and to keep a copy for the mentor for future reference. This copy needs to be easily accessible, not buried deep within the electronic confines of a computer. This is because it's important to reflect on each mentorship and the progress of each student. Between sessions, I like to think about the discussion I had with the mentee and to consider the progress they might be making. There have been many times when this progress has become part of the schoolyard banter I might have with that mentee in passing, while moving around the school or while on yard duty. This is another lovely byproduct of the mentoring relationship and one that enhances the bond between mentor and mentee.

Additionally, I encourage the mentees to use their mentor notes, not just to track their goals, but to also refer back and consider the interactions that took place, and to reflect on the formative discussions between mentor sessions. This reflection assists with the interpretation of the meeting and supports more meaningful action as the mentee works through their set goals. If an aspect of the session is forgotten or needs more clarification, the mentor notes enable this immediate review.

4. Grace and belief

Nothing will destroy a mentorship quicker than negative judgement. One thing I have learned is that we can never begin to assume where someone is coming from. So, be slow to judge.

Let me give you an example:

My father-in-law died from a hideous illness that he battled with extreme courage for 19 months. The day of his funeral I was enlisted to collect the lunch from a local sandwich shop for extended family, the Reverend and dearest friends. This was to be collected following the burial and before the church service. The burial had gone over time, so we were running late, and I was in quite the rush to collect the lunch, enabling everyone to eat before the church service. But on arrival at the shopping centre where the sandwich shop was, there were no carparks. I drove around for a few minutes and still could not find a park. Then a "Parents with Prams" spot became available. I did not have a small child or a pram, so usually I would not take that park, but on this day, given the extreme time constraints, I took the park.

I was only about 2 minutes collecting the sandwich hamper, but in that time, someone had taken it upon themselves to leave me a less than complimentary note under the windscreen wiper.

Dear D*ck Head, Nice F#ck*xg Pram!

Somewhat shocked, I put the lunch in the car and left the shopping centre. It was a harsh judgement from someone who did not know me or my circumstances on that day of such highly charged emotion and sadness.

I like to think that, had the writer known my circumstances, they might have shown a little more empathy and thought twice about the note.

This is perhaps an extreme example, but I think it demonstrates a point: we should never assume we know where someone is coming from, so benefit of the doubt should always prevail. I call this grace. Grace to award a second chance, to be slow to judge, and to assume forgiveness.

As mentors, we don't always know where our mentees are coming from. In many cases we have no idea what took place in their day prior to their meeting with us. If, as mentors, we enter our mentoring relationships with an assumed position of grace and forgiveness, we are starting well.

Our mentees will not always have completed their goals; they will not always arrive on time; sometimes they will not arrive at all. Sometimes they might even try to avoid a session based on their action since the last one. However, if we always approach our students with grace, and an optimistic belief in them, then in the long term they will likely pay us back with best efforts and outstanding final outcomes, and they will have higher regard for our contributions.

It is never about the mentor; it is always about the mentee, their circumstances, their progress, and their aspirations to come.

5. Grit and mindset

As mentors, we turn up on time and we finish our mentor session once the mentor notes have been completed and distributed. We put on a smile, and we welcome our mentees for all sessions. Some days we feel more like mentoring than others, but we know the benefits of our work and we know how important consistent routine is. All the while we are modelling our mentoring approach to our mentees – though there are times when as a mentor we are under pressure. Mentoring sessions usually work within a time frame, and in most cases, we have a long list of mentees to get through. Additionally, as the due date for a project or the final exams are drawing near, we feel pressure to complete aspects of our mentoring work. Then there are the mentee results. Usually these are very good, certainly due in part to the mentoring work that has been taking place, but sometimes, just occasionally, they are not. It is at these times that our mentoring takes a turn as we work through mentee disappointment. This is when mindset becomes important.

Dweck (2009) highlights the development of talent via mindsets. It is all too easy for an individual to have a fixed mindset and to wallow in the disappointment of indifferent feedback. Instead, individuals should adopt a growth mindset; they should see feedback, or disappointment, as a learning tool and consider what was shared and explore the suggestions and ideas for growth. In this way they are turning a potential negative, fixed mindset into an opportunity for positive growth and improvement via a growth mindset. As mentors, we need to help our student mentees to understand the difference and we need to support them to adopt a growth mindset.

Duckworth (2006) adds another dimension to growth through challenge in the form of "grit". Grit is perseverance and passion for long-term goals regardless of the knocks and bumps along the way. It assumes that mastery does not come quickly but it takes time, perseverance and passion for one to achieve what one aspires to. Again, mentors need to help their mentees to understand this and to consider whether they talk about the growth mindset and grit as part of their formative discussions, or whether they consider these methods in their mentoring. These methods of looking at situations differently and building resilience and strength are an important part of the mentoring and personal growth process for students.

6. The learning pit

To further understand one's authentic intentions in the mentoring process and the personal growth we hope our mentees can attain, there is much we can learn from James Nottingham's "learning pit", as shown in Figure 12. The learning pit enables us to explicitly explain the effort process of any challenging academic task. Through six key stages of task challenge, students can come to understand the rigours they work through to mastery.

Figure 12: The learning pit

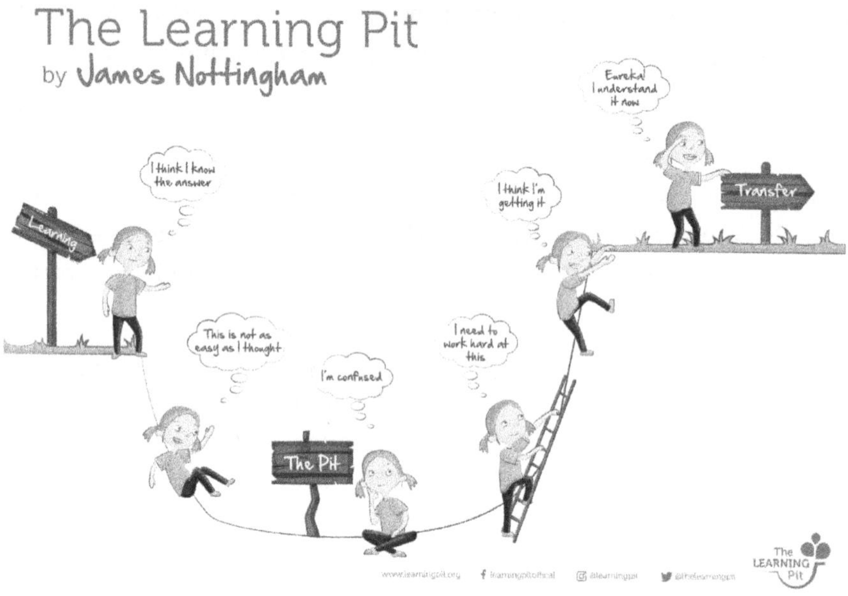

SOURCE: NOTTINGHAM (N.D.).

This is a process that all learners go through, and the learning pit enables students to understand the stages and to identify which one they might be in at any given time of a challenging task. This can avoid some of the blind frustrations that students experience when they do not understand their feelings at a given time.

It is particularly pertinent to the mentoring process, as this can be a point of discussion during formative reflections supporting the student mentee's growth and self-actualisation as a learner.

Transactional vs transformational giftedness

In recent times I have been greatly influenced by the American psychologist Robert Sternberg (2020) and his idea of "transactional giftedness" versus "transformational giftedness". Sternberg would agree that we are life-long learners, but he is an advocate for looking at the practical skills of gifted people and using these expressed capacities as a gauge for identification, rather than relying on the old emphasis on testing alone. He has shared many examples of practical giftedness displayed through one's ability to apply scientific measures such as hypothesising, experimenting, analysing and drawing conclusions, and he has identified developed skills, knowledge, kindness and wisdom as desperately needed traits in the 21st century.

Sternberg would no doubt agree with David Stoddard (2003) that at "The heart of mentoring – Getting the most out of life isn't about how much you keep for yourself but how much you pour into others".

Although Sternberg's ideas do not focus on mentoring specifically, I am confident he would see the strong possible benefits of a mentoring process that supported transformational giftedness and be in support of gifted learners pouring their contributions into others. It is fair to say that "the greater good" is high on Sternberg's agenda. He has presented his "Active Concerned Citizenship and Ethical Leadership" (ACCEL) model in recent years and is now focused on transformational giftedness.

Transformational giftedness is the notion that gifted people become transformational in their giftedness – that is, they see the benefits they have received through their exceptional knowledge and skills, and they choose to use their abilities to better the world first and foremost. This is in contrast to transactional giftedness, where gifted and high-ability people use their gifts for reward or to better themselves personally in the first instance. Sternberg believes that we run the risk of being transactional in our giftedness, something we are seeing politically in many parts of the world right now. A lot can be learned from those individuals who have been selflessly transformational, such as Nelson Mandela, Mother Teresa, Martin Luther King Junior and more recently individuals such as my student mentee in case study 6, which follows.

Case study 6: Authenticity, personal growth and transformation

Amber was an extraordinary international student who was attending the school where I was working. Amber lived with another family from the school, but for all intents and purposes she was largely on her own, living separately to the family in guest accommodation. English was her second language and she had started at the school two years before. Amber's parents resided in China, so she only saw them at the end of each school year.

The loveliest thing about Amber was her intentions for Year 12. At the end of Year 11, she had sought and been successful in gaining the public speaking captaincy for Year 12. She had taken up public speaking a year earlier, initially to help her English language. She was a good public speaker, but there were many ahead of her in terms of skills, so there were times when she was not selected for a team.

Over the course of the year, I saw Amber constantly giving of herself to promote public speaking and to support her peers. If she wasn't selected for a team, she would help the team prepare for the debate, and she would work to find numbers at other year levels where we were struggling to field teams. Amber would do this by approaching individuals and asking them to participate and then offering her support during the preparation. Her level of communication with the public speaking staff was excellent. She would meet with the staff leader and provide weekly updates regarding progress.

Amber was not one of the cool kids, but her authenticity was noticed by others, and her willingness to step into any role to support a team for no personal reward was leading to a high level of respect from her peers. She never missed a public speaking or debating event and sometimes she would catch taxis or public transport to get there. She was always the first to arrive and the last to leave. Amber's life was not easy, but she was relentless in her determination to help others. All the while she was completing Year 12 and wearing many hats to balance her competing priorities.

Mooting was the most highly sought-after public speaking gig among senior students. Usually, two teams of three from Year 12 were selected to represent the school based on interviews and past public speaking performances. Mooting is legal combat in a mock courtroom as two competing teams of three students engage with a real legal case, one team the respondent and the other the appellant. Competition took place interstate and there were a few rounds leading to national finals and ultimately a grand final to determine the national champion mooting school.

Amber never dreamed of making the mooting team, and she knew she would never travel interstate for the moot. However, the work she did during preparation, from communicating interview schedules, to supporting team training, to assisting with trip planning, flights and itineraries during a busy Year 12 year, was inspiring. She was genuinely helping our teams to succeed. Public speaking and debating was a thriving area for the school and one where we were gaining significant outside recognition. This was in no small part due to the quiet and unassuming leadership of our public speaking captain.

During the busyness of the many public speaking and debating events, I was aware of the study commitments and upcoming assessments looming for this young Year 12 leader. The week ahead for Amber at one point saw a debating round on Tuesday night and a legal studies SAC (school assessment coursework) on Wednesday morning, and while this sort of thing happened frequently, the week just past had seen three SACs for her and she was so far behind in her work.

On the night of the debate, teams were short of debaters, so Amber stepped in to assist. She helped the Year 12s to prepare for their debates and then, because the Year 11s were short of a debater at the last minute, and a forfeit was looking likely, which would have impacted the school and its reputation, she agreed to do the Year 11 debate with no preparation. As she was out of age, this meant an instant win for the opposition, but it enabled a debate to take place and it meant that her school did not need to forfeit. Imagine speaking publicly on a complex issue for 5 minutes without preparation. Add to this English being your second language. Add to this that you are studying in a foreign country with no family support. This was a selfless act on the part of our public speaking captain, and it was all done with a smile and the most positive intentions.

Again, on this evening, Amber was first to arrive, and she was last to leave. She had caught public transport to the debate, and she was catching a taxi home. No one was travelling home her way, so a lift was not available, and due to school policy staff could not transport students. On top of this, Amber had a legal studies SAC to study for upon arrival home, meaning she would be in for a somewhat sleepless night.

Such selfless actions were just what we had come to expect from this leader in our school, and following the legal studies SAC I offered to meet with Amber, insisting we provide her with some additional support. Following the meeting, she joined the Year 12 gifted and high-ability mentor group. She was an able student, but she did not qualify for this mentor group on assessment data or grades. It was what had been observed in terms of her practical skills and selflessness, combined with her work ethic, which led to the invitation.

It was August and Amber's grade average was 81%. Legal studies was a challenging subject, but I was confident that with the right support she could do much better. She had been providing so much support to others, but I could now see she needed some support for herself.

So, I set weekly mentoring sessions for Amber. She was thrilled to have been invited and desperately wanted to please. She also felt like an imposter, because her thoughts were that she was not gifted, nor was she highly able. I quickly quelled that assumption. I highlighted that her selfless leadership and work ethic combined with her 81% average grade and English as a second language were enough to tell me that she had some special ability. It was my hope to help her see just how much.

Amber worked extremely hard setting her goals each week, which were around English and legal studies, her two most challenging subjects. We sought out a tutor for legal studies to target the key trouble spots, and I assisted her with her English essay writing and a study schedule. She sought goals around organisation, enabling her to juggle her responsibilities with debating and public speaking, and we largely streamlined her days into what would be realistic and manageable. It was more about organisation than subject support, as she just needed chunks of time and practice, as a highly capable student.

On the day of each new mentoring session, Amber would come with all of her goals met. We would discuss her progress and have the formative discussion about what needed to come next in terms of her goals ahead. She was always so happy and grateful for the opportunity, and she relished the tutoring and the organisational support. She was an absolute pleasure to meet. The sessions continued through September and October, and by the time the study period arrived I offered to continue the mentoring sessions so that she could have the ongoing support during the final exam period.

When the final Year 12 results were released, I was thrilled to see that she had scored an Australian Tertiary Admission Rank (ATAR) of 94, which really equates to a 94% grade average. This placed her in the top 6% of all Year 12 finishes that year and was a big improvement on her grade average back in August of 81%.

In reflecting on the decision to provide this young leader with that mentor support in August, I wondered what might have resulted had she not had it. She was a hard worker, and she really deserved every support that came her way, but had it not come I doubt she would have fared as well as she did. For her, the legal studies and English support was critical. Both were areas where she had some significant gaps. Through the tutoring, these gaps were closed, and she was able to complete some practice exams with great success. These gave her much additional confidence. Additionally, with the mentor support, she became far more organised, to the point where she was organising the day ahead the day before and streamlining her days for a smoother end.

These things seem small, but small things done well and refinements that are made can make all the difference in one's final year of school. This is what well-planned mentoring provides. For Amber, it meant that she could still fulfill her authentic intentions of supporting her public speaking and debating obligations while also excelling in her studies – and personally, she grew so much. She learned a process for subject self-efficacy with the tutors, she learned how to self-regulate her daily schedule, and she gained the respect of her peers, becoming a valued friend to so many.

At the end of the year, Amber was recognised by the school for her outstanding leadership, and she received an award for academic excellence. To Amber her year was transformational. This Year 12 year showed her what she was capable of physically, socially and academically, and it provided the confidence she needed to tackle any area of life with an expectation that she could achieve excellence and success for herself, and also for others.

Authentic intentions

This is about authentic intentions and being single-minded in our approach towards authenticity for best world outcomes. If more of our gifted and high-ability individuals could be mindful of this need in the world, we would be more likely to see solutions to environmental issues such as climate change, more timely cures for terminal illnesses, and greater world equality. The very act of mentoring starts with putting someone else first: the mentee. It demonstrates the importance of others from the outset, for greater-good outcomes and for no specific mentor reward other than the joy of seeing another person develop and succeed. This process displays an authentic intention and highlights that personal growth can be modelled and fostered through the mentor/mentee relationship. It can and often will be dynamic in terms of results, but it requires selflessness and commitment on the part of the mentor and a level of engagement, acceptance and effort on the part of the mentee. Both roles have the potential to develop a transformational mindset for participants – a mindset that can bring about the very best of outcomes, supporting solutions to some of our biggest problems and taking steps towards the healing of a broken world.

Personal growth

If mentors can convey this authenticity of intentions to their mentees in every interaction, it provides an excellent model for mentees to adopt. In the mentoring relationship many mentees are watching every move of their mentor. Their mentor is what they base the interaction on, so the mentor is in a powerful role-modelling position. Over weeks of mentoring and display of such authentic intentions, it is little wonder that we see such modelling mirrored by our mentees. As they achieve more and more success in their pursuits, it is affirmed to them that this mentoring is good and is what they need to aspire to for excellent outcomes. Many of these mentees will go on to become mentors themselves in one form or another, again highlighting the importance of this work.

Mentors not only demonstrate a model for excellent academic outcomes, but they also demonstrate a model for communication, a model for questioning, a model for care and kindness, and a model for celebration and success. This is personal growth, and it is set to inspire a new generation of mentors and mentees as the cycle continues.

Discussion questions

1. From this chapter, what is your understanding of an authentic intention?

2. Using mentoring, how can we help our students to become more authentic?

3. From this chapter, what is your understanding of personal growth?

4. Using mentoring, how can we support our students to grow personally, transforming their thinking?

Where relevant, come up with two or three answers for each question.

Chapter 8

Stories of the gifted

"Student voice is already there. It's not something we give. It's something we honour. And we do when we listen."

– Monte Syrie

"Stories of the gifted" is a forum for student sharing using mentoring support. It came about after many years of working with gifted and high-ability students and discovering the joys and delights of their program experience and progress. I could see that these gifted and high-ability students needed a platform to share their exceptional development as people, their leadership skills, their practical abilities, and their outlooks on life. I knew that much could be learned from such forums, particularly if educators, parents, psychologists and anyone else interested could hear their stories and be provided with opportunities to ask these students questions about their experience.

It has not just been about the positives either; the challenges and difficulties have also been shared and discussed, sometimes in great detail, providing valuable insights to future educators in the field.

Additionally, "Stories of the gifted" is about leadership development and providing an avenue for these students to grow and share their abilities as young leaders opening their eyes to the vast array of applications possible through their learning, skills and experiences. In this way the forum is a strategy for further gifted and high-ability student development using mentoring to broaden the journey.

I have attended and presented at many conferences over the years. Often these conferences have formed the basis of elements of my gifted and talented programs, but usually there is something missing: the student voice. So often we hear from the educators, from the academics and researchers, and even from the parents, but rarely do we hear from the students themselves, the very people we are trying to reach. I wanted to change that and provide a forum for student sharing, reflection and gifted leadership.

"Stories of the gifted" can be shared at a conference, at a special evening, or as part of an educator's professional development day. Students are approached by their teacher mentors and asked if they would like to be involved. Students usually create a short video of 2 or 3 minutes addressing a criterion around their lived experience at school and the gifted programs they have been involved in. The strengths and challenges of the programs are shared by each student mentee, and ultimately the benefits of the experience are communicated. The videos are followed by a short interview conducted by their teacher mentor, who has often been involved in their program for a sustained period. Usually, six to eight students from multiple schools are involved in such an event, and the students share their videos and interviews in blocks of three or four. Shared videos and interviews are then followed by a student panel where the students sit together on stage and answer questions from the audience. The session is facilitated by one of the teacher mentors.

Student involvement in "Stories of the gifted" is initially by invitation, but there can be multiple opportunities across the year. Once accepted, student mentees meet with their teacher mentor at school as pre-arranged. In the first mentoring session the format of the program is shared, and the video structure and criteria are explained. Sometimes, instead of a video, students will share a "human library" – a short oral presentation involving objects, awards or photos of a student's experience (idea courtesy of Michele Linossier). Students will work through a mentoring process as they prepare their stories for the event in the form of either videos or human libraries. Once the preparation is complete, mentor sessions will focus on the interview questions and how these might be addressed according to what works best for the student mentee and best reflects their experience. Come "Stories" day, the students will have been involved in up to six mentor sessions and will therefore be well prepared and ready for the format.

Following the "Stories of the gifted" presentation, the student mentees and their mentors usually meet for a meal and a debrief of the event. This is usually a wonderful celebration of what has just taken place.

Several "Stories of the gifted" forums have now been run. This format started in 2017 and there have been a number of events since then, including a symposium at the National Education Summit, Melbourne Exhibition and Convention Centre, in 2022.

Deep personal reflection on the gifted and high-ability program

For student mentees, "Stories of the gifted" preparation through mentoring provides a unique opportunity for them to consider how the gifted and high-ability program has worked for them in their education. In completing their videos or human libraries, students select the greatest highlights of their program journey to share at the event. For most student mentees, this is four or five things. It might be a completed inquiry project that won a major award, or a collaborative team endeavour such as the Ethics Olympiad, where they played an important part but where they also learned a great deal from others. It might feature a naturalist conference that they attended at Healesville Sanctuary that fed their passion for conservation and action. Alternatively, it could highlight a trip to the Gold Coast to compete in the national mooting championships at Bond University, or a great story that they wrote for the local "Ink about it" writing competition.

In working through what transpired in these academic challenges, the student mentee reflects on the many things that they have done, and they are also encouraged to consider how these challenges have helped to shape their skills and abilities. The whole purpose of such challenges for gifted and high-ability students is to promote their ongoing engagement at school, their self-actualisation, and their personal development – to get them to reflect on their many experiences, and to provide them with transferable skills that they can use in every mainstream class, or in future endeavours they wish to explore. This may also lead to a community focus, or a contribution to a public cause through critical thinking or creative problem-solving action. More will be shared on the latter as we explore transformational giftedness in more detail later in this chapter.

Part of the review of the gifted and high-ability program

For teacher mentors, "Stories of the gifted" provides excellent feedback from individual student mentees on the highlights of their gifted and high-ability program journeys. Where the same highlights come up time and time again, it is likely that that program is a keeper for the future; where the same program comes up as something of not such great value, then that program might need to be reconsidered. Mentoring preparation for "Stories of the gifted" also gives mentors great insight into how student mentees view their program as a lived learning experience. If a student is already good at questioning skills, they may not always choose the inquiry projects stream, which focuses a lot on questioning. If they need to work on their public speaking skills, these students might then choose debating, or a program with an oral component, such as the Ethics Olympiad. If they need to work on their collaborative team skills, they might choose the Da Vinci Decathlon, where they solve problems in small groups.

Mentors do need to be mindful of the choices students make to ensure a good program balance is achieved. Mentors also need to be aware of what programs their mentees avoid, and determine if the avoidance is legitimate, or if it is due to the perceived risk it presents for a student.

An example might be something like the solar car challenge. One of the "Stories of the gifted" students avoided this activity out of a sense of fear. When I asked why she wouldn't put her hand up for it, she stated that she knew nothing about electrical circuits, nor could she ever imagine building one. I challenged her that she might be avoiding it out of fear to succeed, and in the end, as her mentor, I encouraged her to give it a try. I was also teaching the class, so using the student's strengths in reading, research and problem-solving, I gave her the instruction manual and a kit of materials and promised to check on her three times during each lesson. That was all she needed. After six sessions she had built her car, complete with electrical circuit. What's more, as she joined the class late, she had been required to build it solo, which had added to the complexity. However, I will never forget her squeal of delight when she took her completed car out into the sun, placed it on the ground, and flicked the start switch. The car took off across the quadrangle with her chasing it. She then went on to place in the Victorian solar car championships.

This student would never have taken part in the solar car class had I not encouraged her during our "Stories of the gifted" mentoring preparation. This was a great outcome, and it would have been a missed opportunity had the student not done the class. This new skill then also became another program highlight suitable for this student to share at a future event.

So, there are many side benefits to mentoring for a student. However, when it comes to staff who are running gifted and high-ability programs, such mentoring discussions provide further scrutiny of enrichment activities, creative offerings, and the individual programs of students. These interactions provide a valuable avenue for program review.

The value of a free meal

The meal following "Stories of the gifted" events is another critical part of the process. Despite the mentoring support provided to participants in the lead-up to the event, there are still often some anxious moments for participants as they prepare and work outside their comfort zones in determining what they will say and how they will contribute at the event. There can be some stress in the lead-up as students build the "Stories of the gifted" activity into their already busy lives.

However, having a meal at the end of the event is a great opportunity for social togetherness, and a sense of euphoria often ensues. The anxiety and stress that existed before are now gone, and participants can let their hair down to some extent. For gifted and high-ability students who may struggle with social connection, this is a time when I often see them at their most relaxed.

"Stories of the gifted" enables a feeling of accomplishment, and as they have accomplished it together, a sense of camaraderie. Some students speak more freely at the meal following "Stories of the gifted" than at any other time in the presence of their peers and teachers. This is a time of wonderful reflection, but also a time of excellent social connection. Some strong student bonds are formed at shared meals such as this one, and if a few siblings join the meal, or a few friends who come to support participants, I will often welcome them into the fold.

The only essential elements are plenty of healthy food and beverages, and some decent time to celebrate their success. We cannot downplay such times for gifted and high-ability learners as they build their cohorts and their personal confidence.

Case study 7

In thinking about a suitable case study to share for this context I was spoilt for choice, but I decided to go with Clare, who initially participated in "Stories of the gifted" when she was in Year 9. She later appeared again in Year 11, and she sent her apologies following an invitation to participate in Year 12, an invitation she declined only due to her near-impossible workload.

The reason Clare continued to be drawn into this event was the opportunity that it presented for her to have a voice about gifted and high-ability issues important to this cohort. Clare was an advocate for the program, but she had ideas for future developments that she wanted to share – ideas she felt others could benefit from. She also greatly valued the social element of this event.

Clare had been involved in the broader gifted and high-ability program at the school where I was working since Year 7. She was an extrovert with a high level of emotional intelligence. She was highly organised and would plan her school program as far in advance as she could. When it came to the broader gifted and high-ability program, I would describe Clare as a cherry picker. She had a lovely way of supporting all aspects of the program in her response to the offerings, but she would only choose to participate in programs that fuelled her specific academic program, and programs that enhanced her skills in key areas of her development.

Initially, Clare was confident when speaking to an audience, but she was not accomplished in this area, so she chose activities including debating, public speaking, the Ethics Olympiad, "Stories of the gifted", and later mooting as key elements. The aforementioned programs all involved public speaking with various forms of complexity, with her first effort in general public speaking perhaps being the easiest of her choices, and mooting, her final challenge, being the most complex. If she felt that her skills in collaborative public speaking needed to be improved, she would choose the Ethics Olympiad, where she had to think on her feet and contribute to a broader public speaking team effort.

Her decisions were highly calculated to improve her skill development according to what she most needed to craft or refine at that time. I remember on one occasion she chose to do the science inquiry competition for the Science Association, which seemed very out of place, but she later told me she chose that as it focused on creating a working model in an area that she planned to study in Year 12, so she felt it would provide some important background knowledge and a head start for that Year 12 subject. It is fair to say that Clare was big on self-efficacy and self-moderation. Her ability to be streamlined in her program efficiency and to balance her time according to her personal and academic priorities was a strength that I seldom see but aspire to create.

Viewing her cherry-picked choices from year to year, one might be mistaken in thinking that Clare was somewhat narrow-minded and self-seeking, but one could not be further from the truth in that assumption.

Clare had grand plans for the future, and most of these revolved around being a better community service advocate. To be effective in such work, she needed to be an excellent and very logical and persuasive public speaker. She needed to be able to think on her feet about complex social issues, hence the value of the Ethics Olympiad, and she had to have a good grasp of legal cases and precedents should legal challenges arise – hence the importance of mooting. Later this student also chose to take part in the Model United Nations conference, where she hoped to represent China. Again, this was a tactical move on her part. She knew this would bring much turmoil and scrutiny on the day, and if she was to represent her country well, she would need a good understanding of Chinese government legislation and policy. Clare wanted to be ready for anything; not for herself, but for those she would represent.

It was no surprise to me when Clare was appointed a head prefect in Year 12 with a list of community actions and pursuits that made me tired just thinking about them. She became a superb representative of the school and was selfless in her actions. This student wanted to contribute to the greater good in anything she tackled. She truly believed that she could make a difference, and if given the opportunity she just might change the world.

Could "Stories of the gifted" with mentoring support complement models for identifying gifted leaders?

It is interesting to apply Sternberg's original ideas about conceptions of giftedness and the identification of gifted leaders through his WICS model – Wisdom, Intelligence, Creativity and Synthesising (Sternberg & Davidson, 2005) – to the case study above.

Clare certainly demonstrated **wisdom** well beyond her years in terms of the gifted programs she selected to advance her abilities and causes. She demonstrated a high level of **intelligence** in terms of progressing her skills and plugging her areas of deficit through the choices she made. She also demonstrated great **creativity** in the way she manipulated programs such as the Science Association competition to advance her skills in related fields. This left me wondering: did she **synthesise**?

Synthesising is about making connections and putting things together. This includes applying logic from a range of sources. I certainly believe that Clare synthesised in her choices by considering the options, weighing up the benefits, and then making decisions about what would work best. There were no spontaneous calls without great thought. This is perhaps where Clare was an absolute standout in terms of intelligent leadership.

It was interesting that senior students and school staff voted unanimously from 200 students for Clare to be one of two head prefects in the school – something I would have not thought possible when she entered the gifted and high-ability program as a bright-eyed Year 7 student.

Sternberg has continued to evolve in his practical thinking about giftedness and what makes a truly gifted leader. The WICS model has provided much thought-provoking value as we consider who in the gifted world will emerge as an influential leader. Sternberg (2017a) later refined his thinking in devising the ACCEL model of Active Concerned Citizenship and Ethical Leadership.

This prompted me to again consider Clare from the case study and how ACCEL might apply to her. She was certainly **active** in her gifted program choices and participation. She was a **concerned citizen**, demonstrating her enthusiasm to voice her thoughts and ideas at "Stories of the gifted" forums. She was **ethical**, exploring a range of ethical issues in collaboration with others at the Ethics Olympiad. Additionally, she was driven to understand the legislation and policy of other countries, as was her focus at the Model United Nations conference. There was no doubt that she was a **leader**, fuelled by her outstanding public speaking skills, which she had worked so hard to develop. Her peers could clearly see the leadership attributes she possessed, and school staff certainly recognised them.

If I were to consider how many students from my gifted and high-ability cohort could pass assessment of their gifted leadership ability using the WICS and ACCEL models, only a minority would do so. Sternberg provides such a specific list of criteria through such rigorous models, and these rigorous elements enable us to set our truly gifted leaders apart. Therefore WICS and ACCEL are highly suitable models of gifted leadership identification.

It is fitting then that, as mentors of gifted and high-ability students, we have a platform to test these models through mentoring programs such as "Stories of the gifted". Such checks and balances of the enrichment activity selections of gifted and high-ability students enable each mentee to explore the Why (Sinek, 2009) of their choices. Through its very process, "Stories of the gifted" encourages mentees to carefully reflect on their program choices, in the hope that this might inform their Why and determine their measured future actions. If this is not fostering the getting of wisdom and promoting the emergence of thoughtful gifted and high-ability leadership, I am not sure what is.

Key take-aways

The key take-away for me from the "Stories of the gifted" forums is the transformational nature of gifted and high-ability programs and the mentoring process. We cannot lose sight of the impact that mentoring has on gifted and high-ability students over many years. The process of such programs when planned and implemented with purpose has such significant impact. The impact is not understood or acknowledged by many mentees at first, but after years of participation, in multiple contexts, students come to recognise the consistent process structure, and they implement it for themselves. Indeed, one of my great joys is watching senior students who have been mentored for the Maths Association competition when they were young then coming back with great confidence to mentor the junior students. These senior student mentors are now the wise, experienced experts of the process. The opportunity to pass it on or pay it forward for the greater good is very powerful, supports leadership development, and in itself is transformational.

One cannot underestimate the might of an excellent mentor who shows up time and time again, always demonstrates their care and concern, is the first one to arrive and the last one to leave, consistently has the same goal to promote mentee progress, and is selfless in their delivery. Such mentors always seek the greater good and the best outcomes, but all the while they understand that one day the mentee will likely supersede them and their abilities in this rapidly progressing world. This role modelling is transformational on the part of the mentor, and it can't help but transform many mentees who reflect on the experience and take on the same approach independently. These new mentors will approach this task with their own unique personality, their own creative expression, and their own greater-good goals in mind.

Many mentees go on with their own greater-good agendas to make a difference in the world in their area of expertise, and often they are not doing it for themselves – in fact, usually they are not even thinking about personal gain. Their deeply engaging agendas are driven by a desire to do good things and to make a difference in the world in whichever way they can, using their gifted and high-ability knowledge and skills – and some will be exceptional gifted leaders like Clare, our case study example. These students have all the tools to become eminent in the transformational space. Additionally, given the right opportunities, some good fortune, and the right timing, these individuals just might devise solutions for climate change, find cures for serious illnesses, banish world hunger, or rid the world of child poverty. When I think of Sternberg's (2020) transformational giftedness, this is what he is striving for – gifted and high-ability people seeing a need and being single-minded in their actions to proactively address that need using their gifts and abilities for the greater good of society. As a passionate gifted and high-ability practitioner, these transformational outcomes are what I strive for in the narratives of "Stories of the gifted".

Discussion questions

1. How does "Stories of the gifted" provide a voice for student mentees?
2. What are the key benefits for the mentee when participating in "Stories of the gifted"?
3. Why is mentee reflection important in the "Stories of the gifted" process?
4. How does "Stories of the gifted" support mentee leadership development?

Where relevant, come up with two or three answers for each question.

Chapter 9

The practical applications and school-wide benefits of a high-ability mentor program

"One of the greatest values of mentors is the ability to see ahead what others cannot see and to help them navigate a course to their destination."

– John C. Maxwell

Earlier chapters have focused on the different types of mentor programs and their beneficial purposes, but we also need to discuss how these programs are implemented practically into a school-wide program and their far-reaching benefits.

In terms of financial investment, my experience of active mentoring programs in three very different schools, and the exceptional student outcomes that followed, confirms that it is definitely worth committing staff resources to such programming.

Depending on the size of the school, this might require a full-time equivalent (FTE) of one day per week (0.2 FTE) in a small school, right up to five days per week (1.0 FTE) in a much larger school. A well-planned and well-run mentor program that specifically supports gifted and high-ability learners will pay dividends in terms of student and schoolwide benefits. A school could even make their mentoring programs a point of difference in a highly competitive educational market, going above and beyond gifted and high-ability mentor programs to other more general realms of mentoring.

Regardless of how a school chooses to implement such an offering, staff members (as part of their teaching load) could oversee all mentor programs in the school, which could include: competition mentoring, academic mentoring, pastoral care mentoring, new position staff mentoring, and any other mentor program as a school sees fit. With any new mentoring program, it does need to be a slow build, starting small and scaffolding according to the capacity of staff and physical resources. It also needs to be regularly reviewed each term or semester.

Possible implementation of 1-to-1 mentor programs

Once a school has a designated staff member and has committed a suitable FTE, the roll-out of the mentoring programs could take place in a variety of ways, including:

- 1-to-1 pull-out programs where individual students are removed from a class for a 15-minute period at a set time each week, or on a rotating timetable, possibly during integrated unit focuses or during research periods. This could be done very discreetly with minimal disruption, but all relevant staff need to be aware of this implementation, and they need to be on board with the process.
- 1-to-1 mentoring for 15 minutes during student study periods or spare periods. This works particularly well for senior students where study/spare periods form part of a student's timetable.
- Before-school and after-school 1-to-1 mentoring where students report to their mentor in the most suitable 15-minute block for them each week.

- 1-to-1 online video mentoring in a neutral space, with support from the school and with parent consent. Again, this can take place before or after school or on a student-free day. The student might even still be at school, but due to the size of the school and geographic challenges of getting around, choose an online option. This is all about the greatest convenience for the student. Many senior students prefer online mentoring for the flexibility it provides. Mentor notes are then sent to the student as a scanned copy or a record of discussion.
- 1-to-1 mentoring via email. Again, this is done to accommodate student needs and involves ongoing email communication during the week. This can work very well, particularly for some senior students.

It is largely about determining what works best for the mentees and the broader school programs and timetables. Therefore, program delivery will be different depending on the school setting. For senior students, there can be many ways of administering the mentoring, and most senior students will have a preferred mode that works best for them and their program. Wherever possible, it is important to accommodate this. For junior students, 1-to-1 face-to-face mentoring appears to be most effective.

The benefits of whole-group meetings for the gifted and high-ability mentee cohort

As mentoring is completed largely 1-to-1, it is important to have regular whole-group cohort meetings for gifted and high-ability mentees. These meetings allow the mentees to see the bigger picture of the mentoring objective, which enables them to see that they are part of a much larger program and a collective cohort working through the same approach. It also provides these mentees with a time to discuss the benefits and shortfalls of the program from their perspective in an open, supportive student forum.

These mentoring cohort meetings for the gifted and highly able students provide a time to encourage mentees to embrace the mentoring program and their potential as mentees to impact the broader school. This impact can arise through sharing outstanding completed projects with peers, staff and parents in project expos and showcases, as is the case for competition mentoring, or in the academic culture that mentees demonstrate more broadly, as is the case for Year 12 gifted and high-ability mentoring.

With gifted and high-ability mentoring, it is not uncommon for the gifted and high-ability senior student cohort to determine, over lunch, other proactive actions that they need to take to assist their wider peer group beyond the mentoring. Every year this gifted and high-ability group will be considering their broader peers – in part because they know that the better the wider cohort perform as individual Year 12 students, the better the results will be for all Year 12 students in the school once scaled. Additionally, many will likely acknowledge that they have a reputation to maintain, based on the momentum that has been building through past Year 12 results, and this year's cohort also wishes to leave their academic legacy.

A good example of this, which in my view created a real culture shift at my school a few years ago, saw the gifted and high-ability senior students offering subject tutorials to their broader Year 12 cohort in subjects that the highly able students were good at. They then encouraged the broader Year 12 cohort, which included all students outside the gifted and high-ability group, to offer tutorials in subjects which they excelled in.

Once the broad range of tutorials were on offer, the high-ability cohort then ran their tutorials, but they also attended tutorials run by their less-able peers in subjects outside the highly able students' strong subjects. This not only acknowledged the abilities of their less-able peers, but it also built great unity among the broader Year 12 group. Additionally, it removed any elitism tag that could emerge with poorly managed gifted and high-ability programs, and it added in no small way to the prevailing momentum of high-level results being seen by Year 12 students in the school.

The whole Year 12 cohort was impacted by the senior gifted and high-ability students in this unified approach, which further improved the student buy-in by gifted and high-ability students. Furthermore, it promoted mutual respect from the majority of Year 12s across the school. This contributed to an increased sense of belonging and built stronger academic momentum schoolwide.

Through this example, we see what can be possible in terms of raising the academic bar. The academic culture will almost always be driven by the most senior students, and where they are displaying such mature, proactive approaches observed by younger students, the younger students will usually follow their lead and aspire to similar ideas and actions.

It should be noted, however, that such cohort meetings need not be run for the Year 12 targeted mentor group. The targeted mentor platform exists to support struggling students, and therefore it needs to be run discreetly in order to have maximum individual benefit. Each mentoring partnership within the targeted mentor group is unique, and the objectives are carefully tailored to ensure best outcomes for the student's learning deficit, be that underachievement, a learning challenge, or specific support.

Using the mentoring structure to build student agency and broaden academic culture

We see further far-reaching outcomes school-wide from competition mentoring with much younger students, sometimes as young as Year 2. The logical, organised process of competition mentoring sessions creates a clear structure for mentees, and the session progress checks, which serve as constructive formative assessment, set the stage for an outstanding inquiry and a quality end product.

Once students engage with this process, and the associated successes that likely come their way, and when with pride they share their final projects with others through their competition expos and showcases, rarely will they depart from it as they move through the school.

This momentum of student agency builds mentee confidence and forms part of future class discussions and shared peer collaborations, providing direction for their mainstream classes. This again builds learning quality which impacts all students, above and beyond the gifted and highly able cohort.

Students across the school will watch the process that takes place in mentoring sessions. Many will take an interest in the progress of participating students and the quality of work that they produce. The broader school will view the completed projects at the project expos, and they will note the attention to detail and the broad array of topics. Many of these students will aspire to get involved themselves, and good schools will not deny any enthusiastic student the opportunity to take part. Competition mentoring needs to be an inclusive aspect of any gifted and high-ability program. Again, this avoids any risk of an elitism tag, as mentors and classroom teachers support the less-able students as they delve into the rigours of an inquiry project. Some students are identified as candidates for gifted and high-ability programs through their first steps in competition mentoring. These students usually will not test well but demonstrate amazing practical skills, presentation skills, and research skills.

Once the mentor program, with its variety of facets, has been integrated into the broader school program, and an awareness of the program is unfolding across the school, the school will start reaping the benefits. These benefits will only come with a well-organised and well-implemented program and a sustained commitment from senior management stakeholders. The programs need to run their course as planned and with the key goals in mind. A commitment of at least three years is required, but many benefits will be seen even in the first year.

Schools are busy places, and it is inevitable that a week or two of mentoring sessions per term will be lost due to illness, school excursions, guest speakers, public holidays, etc. This is normal and won't usually inhibit the broader program, provided the mentor pivots in terms of the state of play and what needs to come next for the mentee. During these times, the mentor needs to remain optimistic and just "keep on keeping on". The way the mentor deals with these challenges will model problem-solving for life for the mentee. This is life and the way we will inevitably live it, and it will continue throughout a mentee's journey long after they have left the school, so it is important for the mentee to ride these bumps and knocks. Usually very little if any momentum is lost during these mentor program disruptions.

Competition mentoring – practical application and benefits

Chapter 5 captures the structure of this mentoring process in the detail a school would need to implement it. See the mentoring cycle in Figure 2 (page 41) and also the format of mentor sessions in Figure 8 (page 71). These figures provide the structure for competition mentoring implementation in terms of the logistical setup. Further details with project examples and overarching questions can be found in Chapter 5. However, in terms of making competition mentoring happen in your school, there are a few options available to schools for doing this:

1. **Employ an expert mentor for full implementation** – By employing an expert mentor, a school will receive full support in the process, as the expert mentor can assist the overseeing staff member as they work through the competition mentoring process the first time around. Alongside the overseeing staff member, the expert mentor can communicate with the selected students, from that first meeting where the key handouts are provided and distributed. This support would continue as the mentees decide on a project focus and create a suitable overarching question. It would then evolve to the full project framework, with the sequence of questions or tasks being chosen, and participation in each of the mentoring sessions. The expert mentor can support students through the submission process and organise logistics for the broader project sharing or expo. The expert mentor can assist with the assessment and selection of projects for the competition, the setup of criteria medals, and the award rollout process, including school, state and national awards. All this could take place while

the expert mentor works with the school staff member who will oversee competition mentoring in future efforts.

2. **Employ an expert mentor to mentor key staff** – This entails an expert mentor setting a six-session proposal for rollout of the competition mentoring process in a school, and mentoring the relevant staff members. Each mentor session would take place for 90 minutes and could be held outside school hours if required. The first two sessions would take place prior to the competition mentoring commencing, to support the key staff in setting up the competition mentoring correctly. This would involve everything from the preparation of handouts for project ideas to addressing key "success criteria" and the parent letter sent home. Sessions 3 and 4 would take place during the mentoring process, to answer any questions the key staff might have and provide advice regarding trouble-shooting or next steps. Session 5 would take place prior to project submission and would highlight assessment and the project expo or showcase. Session 6 would focus on student selection for the competition, competition awards, school-based awards, and state and national awards and how these are managed.

3. **Employ the methods independently using the advice in this book** – Refer to Chapter 5 for process ideas and advice on how competition mentoring could be rolled out in your school for a range of inquiry-based competitions.

Regardless of the level of support a school chooses, if schools are serious about implementing competition mentoring, and approach this practice with purpose and commitment, they will likely see:

- A much greater understanding of the inquiry learning process and its application through the mentoring of mentees and how the mentoring impact can resonate across the school.
- Improved questioning skills during the mentoring process, with a greater knowledge of this practice permeating through the school.
- Greater interest and engagement in inquiry-related tasks.
- An understanding of the structural process for completing inquiry learning tasks from start to finish.

- Greater independence and student agency among mentored students with integration of this agency into classrooms more broadly.
- Improved research skills and study habits among students being mentored, and a likelihood that these skills and study habits will hold in future years for these students.

When administered well and with all components as per the suggested process in Chapter 5, competition mentoring not only impacts the mentored students, but also filters through to the wider school and raises the bar of academic culture due to the increased awareness of such processes. This awareness is raised via public displays, which include the visual action of mentoring in process, project expos and showcases, presentation of school awards, and the sharing of state level and sometimes national results at assemblies and in other public domains. This success becomes something that students aspire to, and this has been evident in every school where I have seen competition mentoring in action. Additionally, mentored students will carry their newfound skills into their classrooms, impacting their peers in class discussions, collaborative group work, and shared task focuses.

Below are some comments from students who have been involved in multiple competition mentoring programs:

> *Thanks for challenging me, by supporting me to ask great questions that make me think.*
>
> *I have enjoyed doing the extension tasks beyond my first question as they have taken my work to a higher level.*
>
> *This freedom to do research has been something I really like doing.*
>
> – Callum
>
> *Thanks for helping me to achieve "Criteria Met".*
>
> *My session with my mentor is the best part of my week. It gets me excited about my research and new things that I can learn.*
>
> *I have completed projects that I didn't think I could do.*
>
> – Yani

I can't wait to see what I find out next in my research.

I know how to ask good questions now, so I can set my own challenges.

Working through tables and making graphs is so interesting. It can prove what I found out.

– Anna

Students will rarely say exactly what you hope they might in their comments, but the remarks above are an exciting reflection of student experience and new learnings from the mentoring process for inquiry competitions. The comments above, many from primary students, clearly demonstrate the value of such mentoring programs in terms of mentee benefits.

Year 12 academic mentoring – practical application and benefits

Chapter 6 captures this mentoring process in more detail, but in terms of the implementation structure, Figure 2 (page 41) and Figure 11 (page 90) demonstrate this implementation.

As stated before, Figure 11 was taken from a previous case study in Chapter 6 and highlights 10 student goals in the mentor session as were requested by that student. Ordinarily there would be:

- Five goals set for the gifted and high-ability mentees from mentor session to mentor session, and
- Three goals set for the targeted mentees from mentor session to mentor session.

Aside from this, Figure 11 is a typical Year 12 mentor session as it would be documented by the mentor.

It should be noted that Year 12 academic mentoring is longer, more sustained, and more complex than other mentoring methods. When it comes to administering this process in a school for the first time, to see the results that a school would hope for quickly, a school would be best placed to:

1. **Employ an expert mentor for full implementation** – Similar in process to competition mentoring shared previously. This could be done by employing an expert in a school one day per week for the full year. Using the methods shared in this book, a suitably trained mentor should be well prepared and strategically positioned to move the Year 12 academic results forward. However, in completing this role it would be essential for the school to provide a workspace and access to the Year 12 students and staff for mentoring purposes. It would be important to set Year 12 mentoring programs for both the gifted and highly able cohort and the targeted cohort.

   I have recently had this very discussion with a school that in my view is ready for such mentoring implementation. Over the last decade, this school has consistently ranked in the low 200s (out of approximately 650 schools) in the Victorian Certificate of Education (VCE), based on the percentage of study scores over 40 and their average study score. This school has an established history with good staff resources, ample physical facilities, many capable students, and solid administrative processes. I have recently shared with this school's management that, based on these assets, I would be surprised if they could not improve their VCE ranking to be in the top 100 schools within two years, based on the common VCE measures. To do so, however, this school would need to administer a Year 12 gifted and high-ability mentor program and a Year 12 targeted mentor program, preferably employing an expert mentor for full implementation.

Alternatively, a school could:

2. **Employ an expert mentor to mentor key staff** – This could be administered in a similar way to the competition mentoring shared previously, with mentoring of key staff conducted on a monthly basis across the year over eight or ten 90-minute mentoring sessions. Although in my view slower and possibly less effective than the full implementation, this could be another option for schools serious about improving their VCE results.

Of course, the third option would be to:

3. **Employ the methods independently using the advice in this book** – Refer to Chapter 6 for process ideas and advice on how Year 12 academic mentoring could be rolled out in your school for gifted and high-ability students and targeted students.

It is fair to say that option 1 above would likely bring about very positive outcomes for a school where sound processes are in place, including timely assessment and reporting and a level of data efficiency. Additionally, the school would need to have Year 12 staff committed to a culture of improvement, and school leadership would need to allow relative freedom for the mentoring process to take place on at least one day a week.

Significant improvements in results would likely be seen in the first year, with further improvements also likely in the succeeding years. Some of the benefits of mentoring these Year 12 students would almost certainly include:

-   A refinement of student skills, knowledge and application to their Year 12 study.
-   Greater student discipline, planning and executive functioning.
-   A greater understanding of student self-efficacy and self-regulation.
-   Greater cohesion among the like-minded peer group of gifted and high-ability mentees.
-   Greater confidence, direction and process action among targeted students.
-   VCE achievements beyond the expectations of staff, students and historic data trends, due largely to improved study habits, self-efficacy and confidence.
-   A shift in the school's broader academic culture.

Although there are many relational benefits of the mentoring process (Vrabie, 2021), from my experience, the discipline of meeting 1-to-1 so regularly puts a rigorous plan in place that sets the tone for the year.

Students who engage with the mentoring process see results that are often beyond their expectations. Students who meet with a mentor during Year 12 will usually be more organised. They will plan more, reflect more on their assessment feedback, work, and achievements, be more measured and purposeful in their study, and generally strive for better personal outcomes. Below are some comments from a range of Year 12 mentees over the years:

> *The mentoring process made me more aware of what I was going through academically.*
>
> *Through my mentoring meetings I reflected more on my progress than I would have done otherwise.*
>
> *There was no pressure in the mentoring, but I did feel that I needed to be organised and ready for my next meeting, which made me accountable to my goals.*
>
> – Will

> *The mentoring provided an additional layer of support which I found very reassuring.*
>
> *My mentor's positive approach and optimistic outlook gave me confidence that I was on track. Especially because he had been doing this mentoring very successfully for a long time.*
>
> *Knowing what others had achieved through the mentoring in past years meant I had to be involved. Past results were awesome and so were mine. Our school never used to do this well.*
>
> – Sarah

> *I liked knowing that my cohort were all going through the mentoring, as we could compare notes and build strength together.*
>
> *Through the mentoring I did feel that my best efforts were good enough and I didn't feel that I would be defined as a person by my results.*
>
> *At the mentor lunches I learned just how much could be achieved during the final study period. This gave me confidence as I felt a bit behind once all the subject content was complete.*

I improved 12% on my grade average during the final study period. Amazing.

– Tom

My mentor assisted me with planning essays, which greatly improved my essay results.

Through the mentoring, my organisation and life-balance were transformed, helping me to have a much more enjoyable VCE experience socially than I might have otherwise.

I came to understand my strengths as a learner through my discussions with my mentor and the actions that followed in my approach to assessments.

– Lucy

These comments from Year 12 mentees wonderfully capture so much of the essence of the mentoring process. Indeed, there were so many great comments, it was hard to choose between them. However, I often wonder what these mentees might have said three or four years on. The above comments were made during, or immediately following, the mentoring process, but the transformational aspect of such programs, as highlighted by Sternberg's (2020) transformational giftedness, is perhaps not seen or realised until much later. Even so, having been involved in mentoring for two decades now, I have no doubt of the transformational effects of mentoring and its lifelong impacts.

Other mentoring – practical applications and benefits

Mentoring staff into new positions of responsibility is another excellent way of implementing further mentoring benefits at your school. The incredible potential of such mentoring, however, will only be achieved with excellent mentor planning, a well-administered structure that is organised (yet flexible), and when scheduled chunks of time are committed to the process in the forward planning.

From my experience, it is usually best to seek an outside mentor for such a task. With good planning, a senior staff member in the school could potentially be the mentor, but they must have the time to do it well and they must document all sessions for the benefit of both parties. The documentation for each session can be completed on a flipside A4 and should be made available to both parties at the end of each session.

Six to ten 90-minute mentor sessions scheduled a month apart can achieve incredible outcomes for the staff member in the new role when the mentor is skilled, knowledgeable and experienced. I estimate that in many such mentoring partnerships the mentee can be advanced three or four years by way of knowledge and understanding in their new role when they are supported by a suitable mentor in their first year. In critical positions such as principal, vice-principal, head of curriculum, head of house, head of diversity, head of enrichment, head of faculty, head of mentoring, etc., this can be money extremely well spent in terms of the benefits these leaders can bring to their students, colleagues, and the broader school community. The importance of fast-tracking their knowledge and skills cannot be underestimated.

For the mentor, it starts with viewing the position description (PD) of the job and planning a possible mentoring process using that. A framework for the full mentoring plan should be set up, in advance, as a starting point. As I currently do this mentoring in a few schools with staff in new senior roles, if a school is interested in this service, I submit a flipside A4 proposal to the school, outlining my plan. This is done after first speaking to the staff member who has enlisted me to ensure that I have some background context. Once my proposal has been submitted, it is either accepted or a discussion follows to refine the proposal for suitability.

Initial actions for session 1 will usually start with an audit of the position as it currently stands to assist the mentee in gaining an understanding of the background of their new role. This will involve revisiting the school values, its pedagogy, and the desires of senior management as a starting point.

Once the audit is complete, the unfolding plan and action for the role is discussed and then implemented as planned using the PD as a guide. In an eight-session mentoring proposal the planning and action sessions usually run from session 2 or 3 to session 6, depending on the length of the audit at the beginning. Sometimes the plan/action rollout will change according to the varying needs of the mentee and their progress.

Session 7 will usually include a review of progress so far to ensure that all is on track. This might be done using a PMI analysis of "positives, minuses and interesting" progress in relation to the role, or a SWOT analysis looking at "strengths, weaknesses, opportunities or threats". Following this process, we acknowledge all that has been achieved with a little fist pump, then address the minuses in the PMI, or the weaknesses and threats using the SWOT model, for the remainder of that session, discussing possible strategies for overcoming such challenges. Session 8 then focuses on future actions for the plan ahead.

Exploratory or follow-up tasks should be set for the mentee between sessions, and these should be the first port of call in each new mentoring session. It helps when the mentor can be responsive to the staff mentee's progress in terms of the "gradual release of responsibility" approach (Pearson et al., 1983), where the mentor might first share "what they would do" in a situation by way of modelling and example, then the mentor and mentee might discuss and explore "what we would do together" by way of action and solution, followed finally by the mentor handing over to the mentee and asking "What will you, the mentee, do?" regarding the upcoming challenge. This "gradual release of responsibility" should unfold according to mentee readiness under the skilled guidance of the mentor.

As more and more of the responsibility is passed to the mentee, the mentor might then adopt more of a coaching approach (Growth Coaching International, n.d.), using questions to guide the mentee's thoughts and planning. This enables the mentee to be proactive in their personal actions and problem-solving. Providing support through questioning can have significant benefits in that it encourages the mentee to actively reflect on their actions and continue to use questions to guide their planning and progress. This is something they will become accustomed to doing on their own as their experience grows.

Mentoring school leaders for one year can be transformational for the mentees in their skill and knowledge development, and in their teaching and leadership practice. In most cases I find that the growth in confidence and acceleration of such staff into their new roles changes them professionally and greatly enhances their level of effectiveness.

Here is what a few have said about this professional mentorship:

Supportive mentorship has been a transformative force in my journey into the role of gifted and talented coordinator.

My mentor's reflective expertise, coupled with his unwavering patience and approachable demeanour, has cultivated a nurturing learning environment where I feel empowered to navigate the complexities of this demanding yet rewarding field.

Supportive mentorship extends beyond the realm of knowledge transmission; my mentor has instilled in me the confidence and resilience to tackle the challenges that lie ahead. His ability to articulate intricate concepts with clarity and precision has fostered a deeper comprehension of the field and its implications for my work.

Supportive mentorship embodies the true essence of empowering others to reach their full potential. I wholeheartedly recommend such mentorship to anyone seeking to expand their horizons in the gifted and talented/mentorship field.

– Brenda

I have found the mentoring experience provided by my mentor this year to be invaluable in terms of guiding the direction of the gifted and talented program.

My mentor brings to his role a wealth of experience, deep content knowledge in the field of gifted education, and many years of tried and tested strategies which are essential in developing a successful gifted program.

Through the mentoring sessions I was able to reflect on the elements of the gifted and talented program and identify what was working well as well as areas for future development.

The most valuable learning for me was the information provided around flexible programming and how a successful gifted and talented program responds to the needs and preferences of its students, even if this means a revamp of units offered on a yearly basis.

– Kate

What began as my mentor giving me encouragement and feedback about my work – often when I was feeling discouraged or underconfident professionally, or unsure entirely as to whether or not I was on the right track – morphed over time into me reaching out intentionally to ask for, and then relying quite heavily on, his insights, advice and wisdom about my professional practice.

The extent to which my mentor knew me as a person and as a professional enabled him to give me advice that was always incredibly helpful. He not only helped me by taking time to painstakingly discuss big professional decisions in detail, but he also mentored me closely through the whole journey of setting up a gifted education program at a school from scratch. He supported me the whole way through, from providing literature to read, to helping me set up a model and framework, to helping me massage the most effective strategic direction of the program. Additionally he assisted with getting me connected with networks of people also working in the field.

To say that the mentoring has been transformational feels intrinsically obvious. I simply could not have known what to do without the constant and patient co-journeying.

My mentor made me feel safe enough that I was willing to let him see me when I was running as well as when I was limping, and he was always there to guide and advise.

I cannot imagine how inadequate my efforts would have been without my mentor's preparedness and generosity to share his expertise, experience, and wisdom.

The true transformation occurs when on the journey, yet it is impossible to quantify the transformation as it is under way: it is simply the norm at the time. Precisely this is where the mentoring has been the most powerful.

– Amy

This is not just about my mentoring; this is the general power of mentoring at work (Stoddard, 2003), and anyone with a degree of expertise and experience can achieve similar outcomes provided they are intentional, well planned and invested in the process.

Discussion questions

1. Having read this book, how are you planning to use mentoring in your educational setting moving ahead?
2. In developing a mentoring program, small first steps are best. What will be your first small steps?
3. Who can assist you in developing this mentoring program in your school? (Consider internal and external options and how they might assist.)
4. What benefits do you hope to achieve for your students and your educational setting more broadly through the implementation or expansion of a mentoring program?
5. List ways that a mentoring program can support and develop your broader organisational culture.

Where relevant, come up with two or three answers for each question.

Conclusion

Having taken the time to read this book, I hope that it has generated a range of ideas for you regarding what is possible for your teacher practice. The mentoring methods within are tried and true, yet the potential for further scaffolding in the mentoring space, or the development of a new mentoring context, is only limited by one's creativity.

What I do know is that the purposeful mentoring process has enabled many gifted and high-ability Year 12 students doing the Victorian Certificate of Education (VCE) to excel beyond what they thought was possible, and it has given targeted Year 12 students the possibility of a solid VCE pass when they may have thought that it was out of reach.

I hope that you too might be able to support the Year 12 students that you have contact with through a similar mentoring process that is right for your school or learning context.

Additionally, I know that – through competition mentoring – much younger students, many gifted or of high ability, have learned how to ask great questions, conduct great research, and complete outstanding personal investigations as a result of mentoring processes. Many of these students have not only learned how to ask questions and conduct research, but they have also learned *how* to learn as well as *what* to learn through mentoring. Many of these students have then applied these newfound skills in their independent work, extending the benefit into their classrooms and future individual or collaborative research. In this way, these students have become agents of their own learning.

Again, I hope that you can see scope for this type of mentoring in your learning context.

As we have seen, mentoring can extend beyond the students to senior staff mentoring other staff into new complex roles, or through a specific teaching challenge, or supporting a graduate teacher in their first year. The adaptability of mentoring is its greatest strength provided it is well planned, consistent, and fully documented. The value of such mentoring practice is significant for the teacher mentee in their work, but additionally it fast-tracks teacher skills, which again benefits that teacher's students, their colleagues, and the broader school community.

A final word on mentoring benefits

It is perhaps fitting that the wise comment of a mentee provides a final word on mentoring benefits: "True transformation occurs when on the journey, yet it is impossible to quantify the transformation as it is under way: it is simply the norm at the time. Precisely this is where the mentoring has been the most powerful."

Mentoring is transformational. When purposeful and sustained, such co-journeying can't help but change a mentee's approach to work and life. It is often during the difficulties and challenges that growth mindsets (Dweck, 2009) are built. This is when one decides to grow through a difficulty rather than be defeated by it. This attitude is far more likely to be held when a mentee is reflecting on their actions and being encouraged by a trusted mentor (Vrabie, 2021), and soon the attitude can sink deeply into the psyche of the mentee as they adopt the robust and ever-optimistic outlook of the mentor.

Such transformations can slowly permeate from the gifted and highly able students to the broader student cohort, building academic momentum and shared expectations. It is these learned experiences with support from mentors and staff that can move the culture and academic expectation of students to a much greater capacity.

Mentees and students more broadly begin to build greater belief in their capabilities and one by one they achieve so much more, leading to significantly higher individual student outcomes. This is a win for all individuals, and also a win for the school.

It is little wonder, then, that with a unified approach to these programs supported by senior management a school can raise the bar so significantly, moving from a VCE ranking of 100 based on VCE academic results to consistently achieving a ranking close to 30. This is transformational change in action, and I challenge any school to see for themselves just how such transformational change might be achieved in their school setting using a well-planned and well-administered mentor program.

Afterword

I encourage you to not only reflect on all of these mentoring methods, but also to consider your context and to apply these approaches or a new mentoring strategy to your school requirements. Every school is different, and each has a range of students and needs which differ from any other. As practitioners, we need to be creative and open to the way we rise to student needs. Such strategic approaches by creative staff set individual schools apart and can enable a learning culture of safety and excellence that becomes the showcase of an educational setting.

I wish you well on your educational journey. Do feel free to reach out. It is my hope that I might be able to assist any educator or school that wishes to embark on a mentoring program. I can assist by way of active implementation, via mentoring your staff, or through general help and advice.

Best wishes to you and your students.

Mark Smith
M.Ed. Gifted & Talented Education
Email: marksmithgifteded@bigpond.com
Website: marksmithgifted.com.au

References

Academic Assessment Services. (2023). Our range of school tests & assessments. https://www.academicassessment.com.au/

Beery, K., Buktenica, N., Beery, N. (2005). *Beery-Buktenica Developmental Test of Visual-Motor Integration*. Pearson Assessments.

Clasen, D. R., & Clasen, R. E. (2003). Mentoring: A time-honoured option for education of the gifted and talented In N. Colangelo & G. Davis (Eds.), *Handbook of Gifted Education* (3rd ed.) (pp. 254–67). Allyn & Bacon.

Csikszentmihalyi, M. (1986). *Creativity: Flow and the Psychology of Discovery and Invention*. Harper and Collins.

Dean, J. (n.d.). Jimmy Dean Quotes. https://www.overallmotivation.com/quotes/jimmy-dean-quotes/

De Bono, E. (2017). *Six Thinking Hats: The Multi-Million Bestselling Guide to Running Better Meetings and Making Faster Decisions*. Penguin UK.

Duckworth, A. L. (2006). *Intelligence Is Not Enough: Non-IQ Predictors of Achievement*. Dissertation in Psychology, University of Pennsylvania.

Duckworth, A. L., Peterson, C., Matthews, M. D., & Kelly, D. R. (2007). Grit: Perseverance and passion for long-term goals. *Journal of Personality and Social Psychology, 92*(6), 1087.

Dweck, C. S. (2009). Mindsets: Developing talent through a growth mindset. *Olympic Coach, 21*(1), 4–7.

Eun, B. (2019). The zone of proximal development as an overarching concept: A framework for synthesising Vygotsky's theories. *Educational Philosophy and Theory, 51*(1), 18–30.

Executive Coach International. (n.d.). Professional coach training program. https://ecicoaching.com/2021/12/20/coaching-versus-mentoring-whats-the-difference/

Fredricks, J. A., Alfeld, C., & Eccles, J. (2010). Developing and fostering passion in academic and nonacademic domains. *Gifted Child Quarterly, 54*, 18–30.

Gaertner, M. N. (2022). *Norm-Referenced Assessment*. Routledge. https://doi.org/10.4324/9781138609877-REE13-1

Gagné, F. (2004). Transforming gifts into talents: The DMGT as a developmental theory. *High Ability Students, 15*(2), 119–47.

Growth Coaching International. (n.d.). A coaching approach to mentoring. https://www.growthcoaching.com.au/courses/list/

Hennessy, B. A. (2005). Developing creativity in gifted children: The central importance of motivation and classroom climate. The National Research Center on the Gifted and Talented (1990–2013). https://nrcgt.uconn.edu/newsletters/fall052/

Maker, C. J., & Neilson, A. B. (1995). *Curriculum Development and Teaching Strategies for Gifted Learners.* PRO-ED.

Manning, S. (2006). Recognising gifted students: A practical guide for teachers. *Kappa Delta Pi Record, 42* (2), 64–68.

Maths Association of Victoria. (n.d.). Maths talent quest. https://www.mav.vic.edu.au/Student-Activities

Maxwell, J. C. (2008). *Mentoring 101: What Every Leader Needs to Know.* Harper Collins Leadership.

McWilliam, E. L. (2009). Teaching for creativity: From sage to guide to meddler. *Asia Pacific Journal of Education, 29*(3), 281–93.

Morisette, A. (2015). Ironic. https://www.youtube.com/watch?v=Jne9t8sHpUc

Nick, J. M., Delahoyde, T. M., Del Prato, D., Mitchell, C., Ortiz, J., Ottley, C., ... & Siktberg, L. (2012). Best practices in academic mentoring: A model for excellence. *Nursing Research and Practice.* https://www.hindawi.com/journals/nrp/2012/937906/

Nottingham, J. (n.d.). The learning pit. https://www.learningpit.org/thelearningpit/graphics/#classic

Orman, S. (n.d.). Suze Orman praises Jillian Michaels and the power of mentoring. Suze Orman Blog. https://suzeormanblog.blogspot.com/2015/08/suze-orman-praises-jillian-michaels-and.html

Pearson, P. D., & Gallagher, G. (1983). The gradual release of responsibility model of instruction. *Contemporary Educational Psychology, 8*(3), 112–23.

Powers, E. A. (2008). The use of independent study as a viable differentiation technique for gifted learners in the regular classroom. *Gifted Child Today, 31*(3), 57–66.

Psychology Notes Headquarters, The. (n.d.). Lev Vygotsky's sociocultural theory of cognitive development. https://www.psychologynoteshq.com/vygotsky-theory/

Reisner, E. R., Petry, C. A., & Armitage, M. (1990). *A Review of Programs Involving College Students as Tutors or Mentors in Grades K-12.* Policy Study Associates.

Renzulli, J. S. (1986). The three-ring conception of giftedness: A developmental model for creative productivity. In R. J. Sternberg & J. Davidson (Eds.), *Conceptions of Giftedness* (pp. 53-92). Cambridge University Press.

Scott, S., & Palincsar, A. (2013). Sociocultural theory. Education.com. http://www.education.com/reference/article/sociocultural-theory/

Siegle, D., & McCoach, D. B. (2005). Making a difference: Motivating gifted students who are not achieving. *TEACHING Exceptional Children, 38*(1), 22–27.

Sinek, S. (2009). *Start with Why: How Great Leaders Inspire Everyone to Take Action.* Portfolio.

Sternberg, R. J. (2007). A systems model of leadership: WICS. *American Psychologist, 62*(1), 34.

Sternberg, R. J. (2017a). ACCEL: A new model for identifying the gifted. *Roeper Review, 39*(3), 152–69.

Sternberg, R. J. (2017b). Does ACCEL excel as a model of giftedness? A reply to commentators. *Roeper Review, 39*(3), 213–19.

Sternberg, R. J. (2018). 21 Ideas: A 42-year search to understand the nature of giftedness. *Roeper Review, 40*(1), 7–20.

Sternberg, R. J. (2020). Transformational giftedness: Rethinking our paradigm for gifted education. *Roeper Review, 42*(4), 230–40.

Sternberg, R. J., & Davidson, J. E. (Eds.). (2005). *Conceptions of Giftedness* (Vol. 2). Cambridge University Press.

Sternberg, R. J., & Karami, S. (2021). A 4W model of wisdom and giftedness in wisdom. *Roeper Review, 43*(3), 153–60.

Stoddard, D. A. (2003). *The Heart of Mentoring: Ten proven principles for developing people to their fullest potential*. NavPress Publishing Group.

Stonewater, J. K. (2005). Inquiry teaching and learning: The best math class study. *School Science and Mathematics, 105*(1), 36–47.

Syrie, M. (2023, June 30). *Student empowerment*. Portico. https://portico.inflexion.org/themed-resources/student-empowerment/

Thompson, M., & Wiliam, D. (2007). Tight but loose: A conceptual framework for scaling up school reforms. Paper presented at the annual meeting of the American Educational Research Association (AERA), 9–13 April 2007, Chicago, IL.

VanTassel-Baska, J. (2005a). Pre-conference workshop. World Council for Gifted and Talented Children (WCGTC).

VanTassel-Baska, J. (2005b). Gifted programs and services: What are the nonnegotiables? *Theory Into Practice, 44*(2), 90–97.

VanTassel-Baska, J. (2007). Leadership for the future in gifted education: Presidential address, NAGC 2006. *Gifted Child Quarterly, 51*(1), 5–10.

VanTassel-Baska, J., & Wood, S. M. (2023). The integrated curriculum model. In J. S. Renzulli, E. J. Gubbins, K. S. McMillen, R. D. Eckert & C. A. Little (Eds.), *Systems and Models for Developing Programs for the Gifted and Talented* (pp. 655–91). Routledge.

Vaughn, M. (2020). What is student agency and why is it needed now more than ever? *Theory Into Practice, 59*(2), 109–118.

Vrabie, T. (2021). Impact of the mentoring relationship on the development of talented students: A narrative review. *Journal of Educational Sciences, 22*, 44–62.

Vygotsky, L. (2018). *Lev Vygotsky: La Psicología en la Revolución Rusa*. Ediciones Desde Abajo.

Zhang, J. (2020). 70 inspirational quotes about mentors to uplift your spirit. EMOOVIO. https://emoovio.com/mentors-quotes/

Acknowledgements

I wish to thank my wife, Kristen, and my adult children, Jordan and Charlotte, for their patience, love and encouragement while I was writing *Mentoring for Talent*. Writing a book is a significant challenge, and I have greatly valued their ongoing support over the duration of the project.

Thanks also to my collaborators and friends over many years, including my reviewers who have had input as I have written this book. Your thoughts, suggestions, wisdom and insight have been invaluable as I have worked through this highly cognitive process.

Finally, thanks to Amba Press for your support in making *Mentoring for Talent* possible. From early discussions to feedback, advice, editing and artwork, the process has been seamless, and for this I am most grateful.

Milton Keynes UK
Ingram Content Group UK Ltd.
UKHW030937220724
445981UK00005B/325